LAUNCH:
PREPARING YOUR KIDS FOR TAKEOFF

By,
Margie Sims

LAUNCH:

PREPARING YOUR KIDS FOR TAKEOFF

By,
Margie Sims

Published by Wings of Hope Publishing Group
Established 2013
www.wingsofhopepublishing.com
Find us on Facebook: Search "Wings of Hope"

Printed in the United States of America.

Sims, Margie
      Launch / Margie Sims
      Wings of Hope Publishing Group
      ISBN: 978-1-944309-36-7
      ISBN: 978-1-944309-37-4 (eBook)

Cover illustration by Sally Bennett Baxley.

Typesetting by Vogel Design LLC in Wichita, Kansas.

Back cover photo credit: Becky Sims.

To my husband, ROBERT, *who has told me all along that the world is waiting on me, not the other way around. Thank you for the years of gentle nudging to finish the book. Now I want the world to know that it would not, could not have happened without you. I love you.*

To my other ten loves, OUR CHILDREN, *who keep the stories coming. You are our legacy.*

To my LORD, *the giver of all good things. How I love You.*

ENDORSEMENTS

As the mother of 10, Margie Sims has experienced the many rich and varied seasons child-rearing brings. What's more, she's gained keen insight along the way. Margie shares her views on what it takes to raise independent, resilient children in essays that are gentle and playful yet knowing and wise. If parenting is a journey, then her book is the guide you'll want to keep on your night stand.

Jane Schneider
MEMPHIS PARENT MAGAZINE EDITOR, 1999-2016

Delightful and endearing. In a world crowded with chaos and noise, tales from this family of 10 children will help soothe your soul. Take a moment to get to know the Sims family. You'll be glad you did.

Allison Marlow
BALDWIN TIMES MANAGING EDITOR

I commend to you the wit and wisdom of Margie Sims. She is a remarkable woman with a God-given ability to glean truths from the Word of God and apply them practically in life circumstances. As you read her words of wisdom, prepare to be blessed. I am sure she will inspire and encourage your spiritual walk even as she has mine.

Jean Stockdale
INTERNATIONAL BIBLE TEACHER; FOUNDER, STANDING NEAR THE CROSS

Margie Sims is a gift to parents. I know her as a writer, a mom and a human being who offers wise, relevant and practical advice that any parent would relish. I endorse her work fully and have used her suggestions in several of my blogs as well as my book, *12 Simple Secrets Real Moms Know*.

Michele Borba, Ed.D.
EDUCATIONAL PSYCHOLOGIST;
AUTHOR OF *UNSELFIE: WHY EMPATHETIC KIDS SUCCEED IN OUR ALL-ABOUT-ME WORLD*

Margie has blessed me and my family with her words and her example. Through this book, she will bless countless more.

Joshua Becker
FOUNDER AND EDITOR OF BECOMING MINIMALIST;
AUTHOR OF *THE MINIMALIST HOME*

I became acquainted with Margie when I included her profile in my book *Sisterhood of Faith*. As the mother of 10, she writes from experience with her characteristic touch of humor, her family life providing rich fodder to share. Margie offers hope to parents of all ages and stages through the wisdom she's gained raising her family on biblical principles.She has inspired me with her positive attitude through her family's moves, her parenting experiences and her faithful ministry as a writer and speaker.

Shirley Brosius
AUTHOR OF *SISTERHOOD OF FAITH*;
MEMBER OF SPEAKING MINISTRY, FRIENDS OF THE HEART

INTRODUCTION

Because I am often impatient when reading the introduction of a brand new book in my hands (I'm in a hurry to get to the book), I will keep my introduction brief.

For almost 30 years, I have been a magazine writer, writing (what else?) parenting articles for local magazines such as *Memphis Parent*. In fact, wherever we moved, I tracked down the regional parenting publications and pitched my ideas. I was eventually able to break into bigger magazines, and finally met my dream goal of writing for *Focus on the Family* back when Dr. Dobson was at the helm. (His radio show helped me raise my children, after all.)

Still, the desire to write a book wouldn't leave me alone. Every time I made headway, however, I would (surprise) have another baby. I knew a large family was our calling, but I often felt like I climbed a mountain and swung one leg over the top, only to plummet straight down to the bottom as my writing came to a screeching halt. Again.

One snowy day, back when we just had nine kids, my husband encouraged me to start blogging. Once I started, I couldn't stop (except to have my last baby). Every day at margiesims.com I told of the latest happenings in our crowded house. Whether my head was in the clouds or in the sand, I made my best attempt to be vulnerable with other moms. After about five years, it was my husband who first had the vision that the book was already written: the blog, our family chronicle.

So, here it is, after almost thirty years of dreaming about the book, talking about the book, thinking about the book and finally (thanks, honey), finishing the book. I have concluded that you can, indeed, have it all. Just not all at once.

For the sake of clarity, I have organized my stories into five sections and put each section in chronological order. I've also added a scripture to each post. Just as Jesus told stories to illustrate His truth, here are my stories to relay what has helped me to grow as a mom.

So let me close with a story.

"I didn't read my Bible but I sang a Christian song," my daughter, Dorothy, announced as she raced through the kitchen on the way out to the bus stop one morning.

"You know that's not enough!" I called after her. She agreed.

And I say the same to you. Please, oh please, don't let my stories be the main part of your daily devotion. They are not enough! Read not only the scripture verse, but also the section, the whole chapter of the scripture reference. Ask God what He is trying to show you. He will answer.

He always does.

Section One:

FUNDAMENTALS

I hear it all the time: What's your secret? Well,
if I have any "no compromise, non-negotiable"
parenting strategies, here they are…

LET IT SHINE ✦

*Do all things without complaining and disputing, that you may
become blameless and harmless, children of God without fault in
the midst of a crooked and perverse generation, among whom you
shine as lights in the world, holding fast the word of life…*

PHILIPPIANS 2:14-16a

Our oldest had flown the coop. First to college, then the Navy. It had been months since we had seen him, and his birthday was coming.

"Why don't we go see Tiger for spring break?" my husband, aka Captain Fun, said to me one morning.

"Uh, do you know how much that would cost?" I failed math in college, but I did know that airline tickets for seven kids and three adults from Vermont to Virginia would be a hefty sum.

"And it is worth every penny," he said. I didn't call him Captain Fun for nothing.

We bought the tickets. We packed lots of suitcases, two car seats, and one diaper bag. We were a sight at the airport. A spectacle. An exhibit.

"I bet you had to mortgage your house to make this trip," a man in the security line said.

Everyone paired off and we boarded the plane. Eighteen year old Bethany and four year old Dorothy were a perfect match. Twelve year old Ben paired up with six year old Cory for some brotherly bonding. Mary and Emma, ages nine and ten, were inseparable. Captain Fun escorted his mother, who I call Mom Dot, although she really didn't need an escort even at the age of eighty-one. As always, I got dibs on the baby. I liked it that way.

To save money, we landed about two hours from Norfolk. We claimed our bags—all ten of them—and made our way to the rental car counter to drive the rest of the way. Twenty minutes turned into thirty. Forty-five minutes approached an hour. The rental agent assured us that our twelve-passenger van was coming momentarily. I kept throwing snacks at the kids, assuring them that we were not sleeping over at the airport. Captain Fun kept assuring the agent that the wait was no big deal.

After almost 90 minutes, the car was ready. We thanked the agent from the bottom of our tired hearts.

"Now I am totally convinced that you guys are nuts," my son said when we finally arrived at his base. I blamed Captain Fun for the idea, as well as the marvelous time we had with Tiger all week. It was a shot in the arm for all of us.

We returned home via the same route, of course. Same airport, same rental car company, even the same

agent. "Hey!" he said when my husband approached the counter. "I was just talking to my mother about you last night."

"You were?"

He nodded. "I told her that one of my customers changed my life this week by his kindness." He added that he would be going to church on Sunday as a result.

While we were waiting to board, the Captain gathered the kids and told them what the agent had said. "You had a part in that, because you were so patient and well behaved. See the difference a little kindness makes?"

Well over a decade later the conclusion is still the same: whether by speaking a good word or simply controlling your temper, the far-reaching effects of kindness are life changing.

MY HIGH FLYING TIGER ✦

...being confident of this very thing, that He who has
begun a good work in you will complete it until the day
of Christ Jesus; just as it is right for me to think this of
you all, because I have you in my heart...

PHILIPPIANS 1:6-7a NKJV

Motherhood is tricky. You go through nine months of pregnancy (no fun), followed by hours of labor (even less fun), and then a brand-new person appears. Like all new moms, I did not know what to expect the first time, but when my gaze met his, I fell in love. Becoming a mother awoke something in me that I didn't know existed.

The preschool years are endearing. Exciting. Exhausting. I have heard the elementary school years tagged the "golden years" of parenting. I would have to agree with that; they like you and you like them, for the most part. Then comes middle school. Attention everyone: aliens ahead. They transform, they morph, they alter themselves into something you don't recognize.

Just so you know, I have been granted permission to talk about my first born, Robert, aka Tiger. He was a little redheaded, freckle-faced, straight-A student. Then came middle school. As is often the case at this age, grades dropped, self-esteem dropped, confidence dropped. So, I dropped...everything. I decided to homeschool. He needed to get out of the muck of the middle school atmosphere. He was willing, I was willing. We gave it a try.

To my surprise, the first year was fun. For someone who vowed she would never homeschool, I really liked it. Tiger was a natural at academics, and I found him to be an enthusiastic student who liked to learn. He was fascinated by the weather, the solar system, aviation, everything.

"What if we could put lasers in each corner of the yard and then press a button and get all the grass cut in 1.2 seconds?" he asked one day after cutting the grass.

Brilliant, I thought. As long as the dog wasn't in the yard, his dad added.

Then came seventh grade when those aliens again took him away. One day I gave him a writing assignment (my favorite subject). He handed it in—with one sentence at the top and a squiggly line down the middle of the paper.

"Ahem, Tiger," I said. "If you keep this up, you're going back to school."

Fast forward to the first day of eighth grade. "I didn't think you would send me back to school," he said as I was driving him to school.

"You have to be educated one way or another," I said. We had tried one way; now it was time for another.

We sent him to a small private school in eighth grade to ease the transition from home. He had a few friends there and did well, winning the Geography Bee and excelling in Latin. For high school, however, his dad thought the smaller school wouldn't be enough of a challenge

academically. Though it scared this mom to death, I reluctantly agreed.

Freshman year was hard. In the gigantic public school, academics were average and he was unsure of himself. Who wouldn't be? He seemed hesitant about everything from public speaking to riding roller coasters. What's more, he told me he ate lunch alone every day for almost the whole year. Sometimes I worried about him until my stomach ached. When did my outgoing, carefree kid become so shy and self-conscious? It was the aliens, I knew it, but I felt I had failed him.

Playing football his sophomore year brought new friends, and his junior year was even better. His senior year, a new career opportunity opened up, and we began planning a move to Vermont. Once again, his dad was confident he would be fine—that Vermont would fit him like a glove. Even Tiger was okay with it as all his friends were upperclassmen and were graduating anyway. But me? The mom? I worried about the move. (Doesn't every mother worry?) He was over the hump, but I was unsure how such a major change in his senior year might affect him.

But the move was seamless. Within a month, dozens of friends filled our yard on the weekends for bonfires. He met his future wife in English class to boot.

Well over a decade later, he never meets a stranger. As for timidity, during his years in the Navy he got a commendation for his courage in the Persian Gulf. The kid who was afraid of roller coasters is now flying airplanes.

"Is it okay if I say you were shy?" I texted him while writing this post.

"I was the weirdest kid I have ever met," he wrote back (which got him a LOL). "You can say whatever you want."

Middle school is tricky. You go through a few years of unmarked territory, face unforeseen fears. You worry. You pray. You don't recognize them for a while. But don't give up. Keep at it. It may take time, but eventually that kid you knew will reappear.

Just ask my high-flying Tiger.

✦ THAT FOOTBALL FIELD LADY

Whatever your hand finds to do, do it with all your might; for there is no work or device or knowledge or wisdom in the grave where you are going.

ECCLESIASTES 9:10

I was standing on the sidelines at yet another football practice when I turned to the mom beside me to make conversation. "You know," I said, "these practices sure do take up a lot of time."

I had no idea what I was in for.

"*Yes!*" She turned to face me, putting her hand on her hip. "But you know *what?*"

I was afraid to ask.

"If we weren't here, my kids would just be at home watching TV."

I started to agree, but she wasn't finished.

"But, you know, the real challenge is getting them home, feeding them dinner, making sure homework gets done, and they get into bed on time because, you know, I am not one of those moms who is going to throw hot dogs and french-fries at my kids every night. Right now, I have chicken and green beans in the crock pot."

She took a breath. "And in the morning, do you know that you can crack an egg as quick as you can pour a bowl of cereal?"

I don't recall any more of the conversation, but I do remember coming away knowing what it looked like to embrace your role as a mother. Though she didn't come across as arrogant, I knew I had just met Da Mom.

At the time I probably had half a dozen kids. But I was preoccupied, winging it, flying by the seat of my pants and I knew it. The writer inside me seemed to never quiet down, and I found myself dabbling

18

in parenting and immersing myself in my writing.

I don't know exactly why that football field lady impacted me the way she did, but I came to a screeching halt, asking myself how I could better embrace my role. I knew the first answer: show my kids they were my priority by writing only at nap time.

Then came attention to the little things—getting up a little earlier, trying a little harder in the kitchen, scheduling in homework time. In short, I became devoted to letting my kids know they were important to me by my simple, everyday actions.

A lot has happened since that conversation, as I have launched three of my kids into adulthood. I still have a long way to go, but I can honestly say I am trying my best to be Da Mom—it is nap time as I write this, for one thing.

Thank you, football field lady. The day I met you was the day I started doing things differently. Your enthusiasm for motherhood has had more impact than you'll ever know.

✦ BETTER THAN YOU THINK

For I say, through the grace given to me, to everyone who is among you, not to think of himself more highly than he ought to think, but to think soberly, as God has dealt to each one a measure of faith.

ROMANS 12:3

When you have as many kids as I do, lots of folks solicit your advice. Being the chatty southerner I've always been, I enjoy sharing my experiences with other moms.

My ninth baby was the first not born in Memphis. I had the privilege of having him in the great state of Vermont—land of freedom, even during labor. By that I mean that I (the one in labor) called the shots. Now, having ten kids over a twenty-five year span, things changed drastically. When my first was born in 1987, I had to stay in bed, push when they told me to, and as soon as the baby arrived they whisked him away to an incubator, even though he weighed in at 8 lbs, 8oz.

Then, at scheduled times I was allowed to reach in and stroke him through a window in the side of that scary plastic box.

Fast forward to 2007, twenty years later. I was all hooked up (I didn't go natural if I could help it) and waiting to deliver. The nurse asked if I'd like to get in the tub or sit on the exercise ball. Um, no, I told her, I didn't think I could manage that.

"Are you hungry?" she asked.

"You mean I can EAT?"

"Of course, you can do whatever you feel like doing." Nothing I would ever say to my kids, but during labor, those words were music to my ears.

But the biggest shock of all was when the doctor told me to let her know when I thought I should push. Times sure had changed, I thought, recalling how I had a nurse storm out of the delivery room when I told her I didn't feel it was time to push—and with my seventh birth, no less. And the incubator? A thing of the past for healthy babies. Nowadays they laid that little bluish-pink baby right on your chest for some "skin to skin" before they even cleaned him up.

During those three glorious days in the hospital, I had two different nurses solicit my advice about kids. "Is this your ninth baby?" my night nurse asked, pulling up an exercise ball.

"It is."

"Can I ask you about my ten-year-old?"

We both chuckled. Of course, I told her, agreeing that age ten is when they start rounding that corner, exiting childhood.

The day I left that wonderful hospital (I am never ready to leave when it's time), my discharge nurse stood beside my bed. "Can I ask you about my twelve-year-old?"

Again, I laughed. Yes, I confirmed, twelve is tricky.

I am the first to admit I haven't done it all right. It has been (and still is) a journey of trial and error. However, I will begin by passing on some of the best advice I've ever received. My mentor, Jean Stockdale, told me long ago, "When you think you have parenting all figured out, you probably aren't doing as well as you think. But when you know you're in way over your head, when you start each day with '*Help, Lord!*' then you are most certainly doing better than you think."

Over thirty years later as the mom of ten, I can tell you that has been true in my experience. And the "Help, Lord!" place is where I live most of the time.

If you're there, too, take heart. You're doing better than you think.

✦ ORGANIZED SCHMORGANIZED

Be diligent to know the state of your flocks,
and attend to your herds.

PROVERBS 27:23

I have a confession to make: I despise organization. Don't misunderstand. I would love to be organized. But I am convinced my abilities are limited.

Getting ready for church, for example, was a nightmare when I lived in the Bible Belt back when church attire was in a class by itself. Finding shoes and socks that matched eighteen feet was a routine Sunday morning frustration—also in a class by itself.

One morning we were down to the wire and I was frantically throwing shoes out of the shoe basket, crying, "I hate shoes and socks!" when I turned to see my daughter, Bethany, standing behind me, no doubt trying to figure out what her mother had against shoes and socks.

During baseball season, I confess I showed up at the wrong field with the wrong kid on the wrong night.

I frequently got lost—with a GPS.

During my homeschooling years, it took me fifteen minutes every day to find a sharpened pencil.

The constant clutter and chaos can get a mother down. But one day several years back, I learned to let go.

I met a new friend who managed homes by profession. These folks depended on her for anything and everything. We were guests at the home where she worked, and we had a conversation.

"You do a good job with those kids," she said to me. "They are polite at the table and they take their plates when they're done." (She didn't know we had practiced for a month before we came.) "I can tell they are being raised with a lot of love."

"Oh, thank you," I said. "That really makes me feel good. My house is so messy. Every closet, every drawer, every flat surface is cluttered. It really gets to me."

She stopped and looked me straight in the eye. "I have worked in many clean houses where the kids are killing themselves. Don't you worry about that house."

I will forever keep trying to do better in the organization department, but I will never forget her words. Her advice has helped me to remember that while having an organized home is a good thing, it is not everything. Unlike then, I now have proof as my grown kids regularly tell me they don't remember the mess, only the memories.

The clutter still gets me down, but when I revisit the essential elements of raising kids, being organized pales in comparison.

THE BARNEY FIFE APPROACH

*Even a child is known by his deeds, whether
what he does is pure and right.*

PROVERBS 20:11

Can we talk about smart-aleck kids?

"I cannot believe the way some of my friends talk to their mothers," my own kids would tell me from time to time.

"There would be consequences if they talked to me that way," I said. They agreed.

Without apology, I didn't put up with sass, and I had my own mother to thank for it. Despite my five older sisters' insistence that Baby (that's me) never got in trouble, I could remember my mother coming at me with a spanking and a few choice words. Mama put up with a lot of things from her eight kids, but sass was not one of them.

Consequently, I have followed her example. From the first time my kids were old enough to back talk, I nipped it—Barney Fife style—in the bud. But unlike Barney, I had my bullet in my gun and not in my pocket. That is, I had a plan.

Preschoolers got a quick swat on the backside. Again, I got the same from my mom, and it only hurt me in the way God intended. "I don't understand all this bargaining that goes on with kids these days," my mother once said to me. "Why not just give them a swat and be done with it?" Amen.

My school age kids wrote sentences as punishment, and I had my middle school drama teacher, Mrs. Mills, to thank for that. One day I thought it would be hilarious if I put tacks in everyone's chairs. She, however, did not think it so funny and ordered that I write sentences: *I will not put tacks in people's chairs.*

I ended up doing the same with my own kids who occasionally might have had to write: *I will not talk back to my mother.* Thank you, Mrs. Mills, for that very creative idea.

Middle and high schoolers sometimes wrote sentences, but mostly they lost privileges—XBox, iPhone, TV, car keys. There is so much you can take away these days, and so much you can add, too—clean the garage, wipe down the kitchen cabinets, do the dishes all weekend.

For example, when they grumbled about not keeping up with the laundry adequately, the laundry got turned over to the grumbler. End of issue. Nipped it. Just like Barney.

Bottom line: kids have to learn how to be nice, and guess whose job it is to teach them? You win, parents. Teachers can't do it by themselves. Counselors can come up with solutions till the cows come home, but unless we parents take responsibility for our kids' behavior, the issues will never really be resolved.

So get those pencils sharpened. Have the paper ready. When Junior smarts off, and he will, pull out your weapons like old Barney used to pull out his pistol. And, whatever you do, don't forget your bullet.

✴ MY BEAMING BETHANY

The full soul loatheth an honeycomb; but to the
hungry soul every bitter thing is sweet.

PROVERBS 27:7 (KJV)

One summer when daughter Bethany was about thirteen, we were, shall we say, frequently at odds with one another. It was, *ahem*, the middle school years, and those aliens I mentioned before were taking over. I decided I was going to keep her out of my hair. I mean, keep her extremely busy with productive activities.

First on the agenda was a trip to Atlanta to see her cousins. Her Aunt Bonnie, my sister, was the "hostess-with-the-mostest," and showed her and her brother, Tiger, a marvelous time. "Mom," Bethany said when she got off the plane, "why do we live in this city? There is nothing to do here."

A few weeks later, it was time to go to youth camp. Camp was a big part of my life growing up and I loved to send my kids. Upon arriving home, she announced it really wasn't *that* much fun this year.

Next came our church's junior high choir tour. We went to the mall to get the required performance clothes. She didn't like them—the khaki skirts were ugly, she said, and *why* did they have to be so *long*?

It took me all summer to realize that my plan had backfired. The more I tried to entertain her, the more she complained. By the end of the summer, I had created a monster.

"Uh, Bethany," I spoke up when summer was nearly over, "next summer you are going to have to pay for all your activities yourself."

"How?"

"Babysitting or whatever else you can come up with."

"But, *why*?"

"You have been nothing but ungrateful this whole summer."

"But I said thank you."

"Figure it out," I said. (That's one of my favorite things to say.) End of discussion.

The last of the summer agenda was a week-long inner-city VBS ministry. I started to keep her home, but decided she was already committed. I dropped her off on Monday, knowing the nature of this trip was very different from the others. They would be sleeping on a gym floor, working outside all day in the Memphis heat, and having meals like canned ravioli and PB&J for dinner. I wasn't sure what kind of mindset she would be in when I picked her up on Friday. I pulled up and she bounced out to the car, beaming.

"Out of everything I've done all summer, this week had the deepest impact on me."

A full soul loathes even honey, Proverbs reminds us. A glaring parenting principle is hidden here, and every mom gets it. It is the reason a solo trip to the grocery store feels like a party; why fifteen minutes alone in the car line is often the equivalent of a two hour nap. It's all you get, and you make it work.

Keep kids a little hungry instead of allowing them to get overstuffed. Eventually, they'll be grateful you did.

Just ask my beaming Bethany.

✦ LONG DAYS, SHORT YEARS

*To everything there is a season, a time for
every purpose under Heaven.*
ECCLESIASTES 3:1

When the temperature hovers below freezing in early spring, I keep reminding myself that spring is hiding out there somewhere. It will come, I keep telling myself.

Raising kids is the same. You bring that baby home from the hospital; he turns your world upside down. The days are long, the nights are longer. What's more, you cannot anticipate how the siblings will respond to the newest member of the family.

When Matthew was a toddler, for instance, older sister Bethany decided we needed to sell him. I picked up the phone, thinking if I played along she would retract in horror at the thought of selling her cherub-cheeked brother.

"Hello? Yes, I have a boy whose sister has decided he needs a new home. How much? Just a minute."

I put the phone down. "They want to know how much."

She held up her hand, spreading her fingers wide. "Five dollars?" I asked. She nodded, never even turning away from the television.

"Five dollars," I said, trying to keep a straight face.

"Here, he will want this," she chirped when I hung up the phone. Without any hesitation, she handed me his favorite Donut Man video. How nice of her.

I came screeching to a halt, explaining how we could never, no never, sell baby brother Matthew. To my surprise, she was disappointed. But he forgave her for that, and I am happy to report they remain friends to this day.

When I brought Ben home from the hospital, Matthew was three. He pointed at my stomach and said, "I thought you already *had* the baby." It took a while, but I forgave him for that.

A few days later, he wearily asked, "When is that baby's mother coming to pick him up?" I tried to explain that I was that baby's mother. It took some time, but he forgave me for that.

The baby season can be hard on everybody. Adorable? Yes. Exhausting? You bet. But buckle your seat belt, the next season is coming.

Someone once said that when it comes to raising kids, the days are long, but the years are short. It is true. You start out changing endless diapers, then one day your son hugs you and his whiskers scratch your cheek.

I get so tired of cold and snow, regularly checking to see if any new spring shoots are pushing through. I consult the weather app, hoping that maybe, just maybe, the temps will reach forty degrees. I strain my eyes to see if there are any buds breaking through at the tops of the trees.

Waiting for a change of season can be agonizing. But eventually the next season does come. For a very long time, I have continuously been in almost every season of motherhood. Long days, short years.

If you're weary of your present parenting season, hang on. Just like Spring, the next one is sure to come.

 TWENTY-FIVE YEARS

*Let your fountain be blessed and rejoice
with the wife of your youth.*
PROVERBS 5:18

When Captain Fun and I celebrated our silver anniversary, we did it up right—Martha's Vineyard, Boston history, a Red Sox game. First class all the way, my mother would say. These days, we figure every year is an accomplishment, but twenty-five years together is something to celebrate.

"I will tell you what will keep your marriage intact," Mom Dot, my mother-in-law, told me when I was still a blushing bride at age twenty. "And it isn't your commitment to your faith. It is commitment to the marriage itself."

It didn't make much sense to me at first. After all, if your faith in God doesn't keep your marriage strong, what will? The more time that passes, however, the more I have come to understand that commitment to the marriage itself is the only thing that cannot be rationalized away.

Let me be clear: my commitment to Christ is the most important thing in my life. But along the way I have heard people say it is because of their commitment to their faith that they must end their marriage to pursue their dreams. Though there are valid reasons to separate, this one doesn't add up.

Commitment, I have learned, forces you to move forward in the relationship. It keeps you from throwing around the D (that stands for *divorce*, by the way) word when you argue. It allows you to agree to disagree and stay on friendly terms. Commitment calls for accommodating one another, supporting one another, for better or worse, richer or poorer.

"If this doesn't work out, I am losing faith in everything," my dad told Mom Dot upon their first meeting when she had us to dinner years ago. Thanks, Dad, I thought. No pressure.

If my dad were still around, he'd be glad to see that Captain Fun and I are still going strong. He (himself the father of eight) would chuckle to know that on our silver anniversary, we were expecting our tenth child. (We agreed, it was hilarious.)

I know enough about marriage to know two people must be on the same page to make it last. If one spouse wants out of the commitment, for example, there is usually not much the other spouse can do about it.

I am still filled with gratitude to have found someone who will keep this commitment both with me and to me. I am thankful he even went along with me on having so many kids. He is the breadwinner, after all, keeping us all afloat.

Thank you, Captain Fun, for walking this road with me, staying on the page and in the boat with me, keeping your commitment to me. I'm in it for keeps, and I know you are, too.

✦ALL THIS STUFF

But God said to him, 'Fool! This night your soul will be required of you; then whose will those things be which you have provided?' So is he who lays up treasure for himself and is not rich toward God.

LUKE 12:20-21

When the day arrived for us to leave New York and move to Florida, dear friends from church came over to help. Boxes and boxes were loaded onto the truck, along with sofas, tables, chairs, and televisions. By the time we got down to the beds, the truck was filled. The shed was still full of stuff, not to mention the garage.

I found myself asking why we had all this stuff. I had spent weeks sorting it and taking some of it to the thrift store, wrapping it, and boxing it up. My final two days in New York were spent either cleaning or preparing things for the truck. Captain Fun spent a chunk of moving day finding places to store the half that did"t make it onto the truck, not to mention he had to rearrange the stuff that did get on the truck to make room for everyone's beds.

Stuff, I concluded, was running our lives.

We had quite a caravan down to Florida: Captain Fun drove the moving truck full of stuff and towed his car, which was also full of stuff. Cory and Goldie rode with him; I think Cory got a kick out of riding across the country with his dog and his dad. Bethany, ever the trooper, made the three-day drive with sisters Mary and Emma, the cats (Tiger and Stripes), and a trunk full of stuff. I drove the twelve-passenger van with Dorothy, Silas, Ben, Mom Dot—and more stuff.

Captain Fun went on ahead with most of the stuff. Oldest daughter

Bethany and I took it a little slower with the pets and kids. Just as we crossed into Florida (finally), a sudden downpour came, typical Florida weather from my understanding. When I came around a curve on I-95, I encountered a traffic jam and had to slam on the brakes. Bethany was following me and swerved to avoid rear ending her pregnant mother—quick thinking in my estimation. As I watched helplessly in my rear-view mirror, a car clipped her back left fender. Miraculously, all of us were able to pull to safety without a pile-up.

The other driver was very kind—another small miracle—and told us, "I just got out of church, and my pastor just finished saying that sometimes things get worse before they get better."

As soon as we'd pulled over, I called Bethany on my cell. What was my first question? Is all the stuff okay? Is there much damage to the car? Every parent knows the answer: "Are *you* okay?"

Why did all the stuff become so suddenly unimportant? Because the stuff that really matters—family, love, faith—is the stuff that life is made of.

✴ CLOSE ENOUGH TO PERFECT

Where no oxen are, the trough is clean, but much
increase comes by the strength of an ox.

PROVERBS 14:4

We had been in Florida for almost a month. I still had about twenty boxes to unpack when Captain Fun returned with the second load of stuff.

I had arrived with snowboards, snow pants, gloves, hats and mittens—all absolutely unnecessary in south Florida. I had all of Matthew's clothes. Those would come in handy since he was away at West Point for the next four years.

Meanwhile, beach chairs and toys from our lazy summer days at the lake in New York stayed back with the second load. Ditto soccer cleats and shin guards (Mary's and Emma's tryouts at the new school were upon us). I bought new soccer gear and one beach chair since my ev-er-growing belly hindered me from plopping down on the sand. Expensive, but what else could I do?

I wish I could say I didn't really get how I arrived in Florida with all the snow gear but no beach chairs. Maybe it was just pregnancy brain, I reasoned, or that I had too much stuff to sort through because I had so many kids. Or because the day of the week happened to be Wednesday. Any excuse would do, but I knew the real reason was because it was just me.

"It would drive me crazy to be you," I have been told more than once.

The truth is, it can drive me crazy to be me at times. Being disorganized regularly requires extra time and money. Though I am constantly looking for ways to improve, I gave up a long time ago on having it all together.

But I've learned over the years not to get too uptight about my constant state of disarray. It's not the end of the world if Cory had to brown bag it because the lunch boxes didn't make it onto the first truck. (I replaced the girls' lunch boxes but somehow forgot about his). It's okay if I had to pick up a few necessities because I left many essentials in New York. I cooked our first few meals without a spatula, for instance.

I have known people who have a hard time accepting anything less than perfection. But I find a lot of freedom in embracing life at a less than perfect pace. I accept it, laugh at myself, and keep living.

Life goes on. As long as I can always find my sanity, that's close enough to perfect for me.

✦ NEW BABIES 101

Behold, children are a heritage from the Lord; the fruit of the womb is a reward. Like arrows in the hand of a warrior, so are the children of one's youth. Happy is the man who has his quiver full of them; they shall not be ashamed, but shall speak with their enemies in the gate.

PSALM 127:3-5

By the time Hope was six weeks old, I had fallen in love for the tenth time.

There's nothing like a new baby. Without fail they remind me how brief time is. Because I thought I wouldn't have any more after Silas (number nine), I realized more than ever what a gift Hope was. I cried when she smiled, squealed with delight when she cooed. I spent a lot of hours in the rocking chair. Many nights, in fact, I inhaled the scent of her head over and over like an addict.

Having a new baby always gave me ample time to ponder the first few months of mothering, to narrow down what I considered the essentials. So here they are. Some advice has been passed along to me, the rest I have figured out on my own. After all, I've had lots of time to think about it.

Baby Advice: Top Ten from a Mom of Ten

10. Get an epidural or other anesthesia if you need it. Eight out of ten times I have been induced. Eight out of ten times I have had an epidural. Ten out of ten times I have needed one.

9. Take advantage of the overnight nursery while you're at the hospital. Like the nurse so knowingly said, it is the only time a new mom will get to sleep.

8. Bathe the baby every evening. I learned this from my own mom (mother of eight) when I moved in with her for three days after I had my first baby. She believed a bath in the evening relaxes the baby and sends a signal that bedtime is near. I have followed her advice with all ten, and I agree.

7. Accept all the help offered. Ask for help if it isn't offered. My church family and a few friends volunteered food—ridiculous amounts of food—for two weeks after I came home. I froze half and over a month later I still had meals in the freezer.

6. Keep the baby home for a month. Just solid, common sense advice. Walmart, Sam's Club, and even Target will go on without you.

5. Nap when the baby naps, then get done whatever you can. (A mentor of mine passed on the advice to try and make your bed every day. Since the bed takes up most of the room, she said, making it every day will give you a sense of accomplishment even if that is all you get done.)

4. No screens for infants. There are dozens of studies out there that show face to face time is crucial to healthy brain development.

3. A no-nonsense nurse simplified feedings for me with my first baby: wake the baby for feedings during the day; let him wake you during the night. This worked for all ten of my babies.

2. Allow siblings to help and play with the baby. Dorothy liked to pick out Hope's clothes, and Silas liked to give her horseback rides on all fours (with my assistance, of course). How many Sims kids did it take to give Hope a bath? Six was the record.

1. Live in the moment. This is hard with the first one, and it has taken me a long time to master. However, with my last two babies, I cleared my schedule for a year. Apart from working in the nursery once a month because I was nursing anyway, I did no volunteering, no manuscript deadlines, no ministry responsibilities. It was so freeing to take the pressure off, I should have done it sooner. It took me three babies just to learn to relax, and six to really let things go.

With the tenth? I was nothing but a noodle.

✳ A WHOLE, ENTIRE, COMPLETE DAY OFF

*...that they admonish the young women to love
their husbands, to love their children...*

TITUS 2:4

"What do you want for Mother's Day?" Captain Fun asked me one early May evening after family devotions.

The answer came easily and was always the same. "A whole, entire, complete day off...from the baby." This time, it was Hope.

I adored Hope. In fact, the more kids I had, the more precious those early childhood years became. But as I often told the ladies at local MOPS groups, I had been home with little children from newborns to preschoolers for twenty-seven years, and sometimes I felt like I was about to die from exhaustion.

But then Mother's Day would come (hallelujah), and relaxation was forced upon me. My kids wouldn't let me do the dishes. They practically tackled me if they caught me carrying laundry to the laundry room. Bethany put the baby down for a nap, and someone else got her up. Don't dare let Captain Fun catch anyone asking me to do anything for them on that day.

Over the course of the day, I received roses, chocolate, a gift card to Bonefish Grill, shampoo, makeup, lotion, coffee, and many other gifts that make a mother feel appreciated.

Then there were the cards. *Oh, the cards.*

"You are so patient." "You don't complain." "You cook such elaborate meals." "The older I get, the more I understand all you've done for us."

"You're a great listener." "You're smart." "You're funny." "Thank you for taking care of us." "Thanks for all you did for me while I was growing up." "Thank you." "Thank you." "Thank you."

Many years ago I worked part time for the US Postal Service. Two young kids would come in to see me almost every time I was at that little post office. One of them even started calling me Mama. Their teeth were rotten, their clothes were dirty, their hair was greasy and tangled, and they were often eating candy for breakfast. Why? Because their mother wasn't there to wash their clothes, brush their teeth, comb their hair, or forbid candy at 8:00 in the morning.

Seeing those kids regularly for several years taught me something. It taught me not to underestimate my role, my significance, my importance in the lives of my children. Those million things I did every day? *They mattered.*

I love a day off. It is what all mothers want on Mother's Day, really. An official, intentional, real live day off. On Mother's Day, I get one. If you're a mom, I hope you get one, too.

But the next day (and the next, and the next) when we all hit the floor running again, remember with me why we do what we do. Don't lose sight of the significance of those million little things we do every day.

What a difference they make.

✦ MARY'S EPIPHANY

And whatever you do, do it heartily, as to the Lord and not to men, knowing that from the Lord you will receive the reward of the inheritance; for you serve the Lord Christ.

COLOSSIANS 3:23-24

Ever since our Mary was in first grade, she has been a runner.

She spent first through fifth grades in Vermont, where she had a wonderful UVM student as her track coach. The program gave her a solid foundation as well as a lot of fun. Bravo to college students who volunteer their time coaching kids.

We then moved to a tiny upstate New York town for her sixth and seventh grade years. Her new coach was the perfect mix of inspiration and discipline for middle school girls. It was there that Mary had her first epiphany: Being lazy is harder than working hard. Do what the coach says, and it will pay off.

Our year in Florida for her eighth grade year meant another track coach, but she was up for trying. She not only succeeded in track and swimming, but also was one of only two girls to make the coed soccer team. Much to her surprise, she finished her eighth grade year as Female Scholar Athlete—quite an accomplishment for a brand-new student.

In Virginia, Mary was on the indoor track team at the local high school. But this wasn't just any high school; this high school was named by Newsweek as one of the top high schools in the nation. Though the school was only six years old, excellence had quickly become the norm. Opportunity abounded in sports, music, academics and everything else. But the atmosphere was often intimidating.

One Friday night before her track meet on Saturday, she came to a conclusion. "Mom, I am not exactly sure how to please my coach—he is a little tough to read. So, I think I will just run to please God." Her confidence was shaky about the four events in which she was entered, but I was happy that she knew that the Lord would be pleased with her best effort.

I am not one to claim that our best attempt at being good can make us good enough for God. If that were true, the Bible says in Galatians 2:21, then Christ died for nothing. It is after Christ redeems us that God asks for our best effort at glorifying Him. That is just what Mary offered Him, and He blessed it.

Long Jump, First Place: Mary Sims

55m Hurdles, First Place: Mary Sims

500m Dash, First Place: Mary Sims

On the 4x400 relay, Mary's team was in last place when the baton was placed into her hand. She remembered the coach's instructions and found herself in first place at the finish line.

"You really can do all things through Christ!" I texted her from Silas's basketball practice when her dad called me with the results.

"Most definitely!" she wrote back.

Trying and trusting—it really is enough.

May we never, ever forget it.

✦ TOP TEN ESSENTIALS FOR A HAPPY FAMILY

Let love be without hypocrisy. Abhor what is evil. Cling to what is good. Be kindly affectionate to one another with brotherly love, in honor giving preference to one another; not lagging in diligence, fervent in spirit, serving the Lord; rejoicing in hope, patient in tribulation, continuing steadfastly in prayer; distributing to the needs of the saints, given to hospitality. Bless those who persecute you; bless and do not curse. Rejoice with those who rejoice, and weep with those who weep. Be of the same mind toward one another.

ROMANS 12:9-16a

Every time a new year is staring me in the face, it prompts me to turn reflective and review my approach to motherhood. Consequently, over the years I have compiled my top ten of, well, everything. Here is my list of no compromise essentials for a happy family.

10. A Clean(ish) Orderly(ish) House. This is last on my list because, while it certainly helps, it is just not as crucial as most people think. Someone told me once that they keep their house clean enough to be healthy and messy enough to be happy. It became my new motto.

9. Be Flexible. Home is where you learn how to get along with people—the give and take, the ebb and flow. If you can instill compromise in your kids at home, you are instilling it for their classrooms, college roommates, the workforce, and marriage. A frequent reminder that no one is right all the time is a good thing.

8. Fun. This is my husband's department, hence the nickname Captain Fun. When we lived in Vermont and upstate New York, he forced me outside to play in the snow. When we lived in Florida, he dragged us all to the beach almost every weekend, God bless him. (We won't live here forever, he said, and he was right.) During our first few months in Virginia, we went apple picking, fireworks watching, hiking, zooing, boating, and to at least two museums. We all readily admit our family would not be the same without the Captain's nose for fun.

7. Perseverance. One of the first magazine articles I ever wrote was called "No Quitting in the Middle," though the editor renamed it "Built to Last," and it is still out there in cyber-land. The gist of it was that once you start something, be it a board game or a soccer season, you finish it. I hope that as they move on to bigger things like careers and marriage, they will keep that commitment to, well, commitment.

6. Share the work. Every night as dinner ended, someone usually asked, "Is it boys' night or girls' night?" They took turns with the dishes, Ben took out the trash, Emma unloaded the dishwasher, Cory cut the grass, Mary changed the litter box, Dorothy sorted the silverware, and Silas picked up after baby Hope. Each one oversaw keeping order in one room of the house, besides their own. Yes, I still did most of the work, but instilling a sense of family responsibility is crucial. (Mom Dot would fuss at me

if I failed to tell you that she folded all of the laundry.)

5. Follow the Rules. Rules are our friends, I told my children from the time they were very young. If the sign says *wet paint*, don't touch it; don't sneak food into the theater,; cell phones sleep in my room and, no, it's not okay for parents to host underage drinking. It's i-l-l-e-g-a-l, and there's a reason for that. Keep the rules and the rules will keep you.

4. Grace. Grace is defined as a sense of propriety and consideration for others. It's the standard at our house. If you want Mom to turn into a freight train, just call one of your siblings stupid or tell them to shut up. Home is a place where mistakes are allowed, and we stick together because we are a family. As Mama used to say, "If you can't say something nice…"

3. Peace. The Captain and I agreed long ago that we would keep arguments out of earshot of the kids. "You and Dad make it look so easy," Bethany once told me. After twenty-seven years of marriage it has gotten easier, but it was challenging at times when we were younger and still getting to know each other. But we have an agreement and try very hard to keep it: kids deserve a peaceful home.

2. Clear Roles. Parents are parents, kids are kids; don't confuse the two. A happy home requires parents who aren't trying to be the kids (or the kids' best friends). Kids cannot raise themselves, therefore making parents a necessity.

1. Faith. I became a Christian when I was nine years old—and by that I mean nothing less than trusting Christ to save me because I cannot save myself. Being a good person to get into Heaven has never made sense to me. (Galatians 2:21, "If righteousness is obtained by keeping the law, then Christ died in vain.") Just about every night before bed (and I give the Captain full credit for this) our family gathers and reads a portion of Scripture. Mom Dot says it is the very foundation of the Sims family. Agreed.

Daily, and without apology, we teach our children that faith in Christ is everything. We uphold Him as the bedrock of our household; not just a reason, but as *the* reason for our happy family.

44

THE FREIGHT TRAIN

Children obey your parents in the Lord, for this is right. 'Honor your father and mother,' which is the first commandment with promise: 'that it may be well with you and you will live long on the earth.'

EPHESIANS 6:1-3

Are we parents really supposed to be in charge? We are. "... *for this is right,*" Ephesians 6:1 reminds us. Bring on the freight train.

Do your kids ever ignore you?

"Come to dinner." Nobody moves.

"Do your homework." Stillness.

"Okay, everybody, let's clean up." Everyone acts as if you do not exist.

In the past, I would repeat requests until I found myself stomping around the house, yelling about why no one listened to me. But now, the freight train comes.

What, exactly, is the freight train?

If you're a mother, you will recognize it. It's that gradual out of control feeling you get when your kids aren't listening. The more they ignore you, the faster it comes flying down the tracks. I discovered that if I began to announce the arrival of the freight train when I felt it speeding toward the station, my kids got it.

"Come to dinner." Nothing. "I think I hear the freight train," I'd say.

"Do your homework." Nobody moved. "I can see the smoke."

"Okay, everybody!" I announced after dinner. "Seven minute clean up." Ignore. Ignore. Ignore. "If you don't want the freight train to pull into the station, you better get moving. Now."

The instant I mentioned the smoke, the lights, the sound of the *clackity-clack* down the track, they understood this was their warning. It was not "The Little Engine That

Could." Nor was it Thomas the Tank Engine. It was The Freight Train.

And a freight train cannot be ignored.

THE POWER OF PRESENCE

Strength and honor are her clothing;
she shall rejoice in time to come.

PROVERBS 31:25

As the mom of ten, I get one question a lot: *What is your secret?* Over the years, it has caused me to reflect on what, exactly, *is* my secret.

My daughters told me sometimes of babysitting jobs or their friends' moms who would say, "I would like to know how your mom stays organized," or "I want to follow your mom around the house just for one day and watch her."

Everyone who knows me knows that organizing is a struggle, not a strength for me. During my homeschooling years, for instance, it took me fifteen minutes to find a sharpened pencil. Daily.

I am not a great cook, nor does any woman envy my decorating skills. The only time my whole house is clean is when I'm selling it.

As for academia, forget it. My recent re-read through my high school and college journals was a harsh reminder. From January, 1983 (my senior year in high school) until I had my first baby, I journaled nearly every day. I wrote down almost every conversation, in detail, that my husband and I ever had from the first time I saw him until the day we married.

In college, I also recorded my grades—somewhat regrettably.

Dear Journal, I made a 62 on my Geography test, but at least I passed.

Dear Journal, I failed my math exam. The only solution to that is ice cream, so I am in the cafeteria eating a sundae.

Dear Journal, I failed my math

class. My dad said if it weren't for the failures, the successes wouldn't mean anything. That made me feel a little better.

I kept all my elementary and middle school report cards, too. Two D's in health in seventh grade. ("How do you make two D's in health?" my children asked me.) And I never got past consumer math in high school. You get it: I am not an intellectual.

Recently when I came down with a high fever, I was able to identify my secret. Not sure what it was that hit me, but I was in bed for three days. On the morning of the fourth day, I finally recovered. As is my usual practice, I crept downstairs at 5:15 A.M., turned on my coffee and said my morning prayers.

As I settled into my chair with my Bible after getting my coffee, I heard Emma padding down the dark hallway. "Mom?"

"Yeah?" I answered.

"You're back!" she exclaimed. "For three days I have been saying 'Mom,' and nothing. No answer. But there you are."

Soon I made my way to the kitchen to start on breakfast and pack a lunch (or five). Cory came down. "Mom, you're back!"

Dorothy was next to appear. "Mom, you're here. Oh, I'm so glad to see you."

An hour later, Silas brought it home. "You're up! While you were sick, I forgot my lunch and didn't get my homework done and everything was all wrong. Nothing was right."

Contrary to latest parenting trends, kids cannot raise themselves. They need our guidance, our love and, more than ever, our presence.

But lest you moms think I did presence perfectly, allow me a confession: I did not. My kids would call me on my "fake laugh" when they thought I was not truly listening. I battled distraction daily.

But real presence, even if never completely perfected, is simple, yet powerful. It holds more influence than money, talent, intellect, or youthful vigor. I was down for three days and my children *noticed*.

When I reached the halfway point of this parenting journey, about to launch my sixth child, I did a lot of reflecting and asking myself, what is the secret sauce in raising kids?

If I must narrow it down to just one thing: Presence. That's it. Just being awake, around, available.

Nothing can compare to it. Nothing can replace it.

UN-CODDLING YOUR KIDS

*Now no chastening seems to be joyful for the present, but
painful; nevertheless, afterward it yields the peaceable fruit of
righteousness to those who have been trained by it. Therefore,
strengthen the hands which hang down, and the feeble knees,
and make straight paths for your feet, so that what is lame
may not be dislocated, but rather be healed.*

HEBREWS 12:11-13

"Coddled Kids Crumble" was the title of the article that caught my eye recently on Facebook. Being the mom of ten, coddling kids has never been an issue with me. Quite the opposite, in fact. Consequently, I confess I have had a touch of mom guilt here and there over the years. Maybe I was requiring too much of them.

But no more. As the title implies, coddling kids is the equivalent of crippling them. After ten years of this faulty philosophy which has robbed a whole generation of problem-solving skills, college kids are limping to their school counselors over the most trivial issues. Some students have even called 911 when they spotted a mouse in their dorm.

There were many times when I wanted to do everything for my kids—their dad was much better than I am at instilling independence. It was easier, I rationalized, and things got done faster. But as this piece so eloquently explained, helicopter parenting and constant hand holding creates kids who lack coping skills.

When Silas was about eight, for instance, he rode with me for the afternoon carpool. We took along a stack of movies and books that had to be returned. "Silas," I said, "take this stack of books over there and drop them in the book drop."

The stack went up to his chin. (It was adorable.) He balanced it all the way up the sidewalk, then stopped in front of the book drop. I could

49

tell he was trying to figure out how to get the pile into the book drop. After a few seconds, he put the pile down on the ground (i.e., he solved the first problem), then opened the chute with one hand and stretched out his other hand to pick up the first book from the top of the pile. For some reason, he seemed to think he had to hold the chute open while he was reaching for the book. It was a stretch, literally, but he did get the first book in, then another, and another.

The whole process took about five minutes, and I confess I was a little anxious to get going. I still had to stop at the drugstore, after all, and Cory would be done with football practice soon. But it was what he did after the deed was done that was so rewarding to watch. As he turned and walked away from the book drop, he hopped up onto the brick wall, trotted on tip toe along the concrete path, and leaped off. The look on his face said it all: *I did it.*

"I am proud of you, Silas, for the way you solved that problem," I told him later.

He beamed. "I wasn't sure how to do it at first, but I figured it out."

Just as I suspected.

When my older kids were growing up, I did not realize the importance of letting them do every day errands like this. Because I always had a baby or toddler (or both) in the car seat, they helped me out of necessity. It was easier on me to let them do it.

But, the article said, after a decade of helicopter parenting, we have a helpless generation on our hands, and they are imploding at the slightest resistance.

"I walked four miles to school across the Arkansas prairie," Mom Dot often tells my kids. While I cannot imagine my children walking four miles to school one way, I think her generation had something the younger generations are missing. Toughness, tenacity, and the ability to rise to the challenge.

When my youngest was on her last year at home before kindergarten came calling, I was down to six kids at home. With no baby to constantly tend to, a new parenting season was upon me. I decided I was going to do my best not to coddle the kids on the other end of my ten, but to grant them the gift that every child deserves—independence.

They're going to need it later.

STORMING THE CASTLE ✦

When I was a child, I spoke as a child, I understood
as a child, I thought as a child; but when I became a
man, I put away childish things.

I CORINTHIANS 13: 11

In 2017, the Captain and I launched child #6 into the world—our daughter, Emma, was off to the Coast Guard Academy.

If there is one thing I have learned about the American military academies, it is this: it is hard to get into them and hard to get out of them. The application process is a long, grueling series of forms, interviews, essays, tests and health clearances. If you get accepted (and only a fraction of the kids who apply get in) you report for basic training (Swab Summer) when summer has barely begun. This is followed by a grueling academic year. After much working and waiting, Emma reported in June, 2017. We were so proud.

Soon after, the rest of the family relocated to Alabama, so we needed to work out logistics of her departure. Captain Fun is definitely the one who finds the fun at our house, but he has another side to him. When there is a big, scary mountain in front of you, he is the go-to guide—a real climbing companion who pays attention to detail and isn't afraid to ask questions. Still, he offered for me to take Emma, in case we wanted to make it a mother-daughter thing.

But Emma was clear. "I need the more expressive parent to drop me off," she said. "Mom will just wave as I get out of the car and say, 'Have fun storming the castle.'" I laughed, but I hate to admit it was true. I'm not a crier when it comes to milestones and goodbyes. Consequently, I can come across as quite placid at times that call for some emotion.

In fact, the day I dropped off Hope (my last one) for her first day of kindergarten, I didn't shed a tear. (Neither did she, so that was a plus). "I like to think of myself as a softer version of Marilla Cuthbert (from Anne of Green Gables)," I wrote Emma in my first letter to her, hoping that was a good thing.

At summer's end, Emma started class at the USCGA. Her sister, Mary, was one year ahead of her, and I was so thrilled those girls were reunited. Being the youngest of eight kids myself, six of us girls, I believe you should be with your sister for as long as possible. One day you could likely end up on the opposite sides of the country, if not the world.

Emma stormed the castle, just as her sister, Mary, had the previous year. In fact, all of our grown children had stormed their own castles, resulting in six kids in five states. Counting Emma, five of them started new schools that fall.

Soon after, I was encouraging thirteen-year-old Dorothy to try out for the sailing team at her new school. "There is a clinic for beginners," I told her, "and I know it is scary, but…"

Here, she interrupted me. "Fear doesn't matter in this family," she said, recalling how her dad signed her up to go to an arts camp only three days after we arrived in Alabama. She was scared, but she went. She said it was life changing, and I was so proud for her.

For thirty years I had preschoolers, but as I mentioned, that season finally ended in 2017. While I knew I wouldn't miss repeatedly having my writing time interrupted, what I missed the most was fixing lunch during their TV time, then reading them a story or two before nap. One of Hope's favorites was "The Three Little Pigs," and no matter which version I picked up, the story always went something like this:

Once upon a time there were three little pigs who lived with their mother. One night as they squeezed around the dinner table, their mother said, "Boys, it is getting too crowded in here. It is time for you to go out on your own."

"You are right," they said. So they packed their things and set out on their own.

I think I have finally figured out why I don't cry over these milestones. When kids grow up and leave you, it is the natural order of things. With a hug and a wave, you say, "Use your head, but have fun storming the castle."

As we made the final turn into the school that morning, I asked Hope how she was doing. "I'm nervous, but I'm brave," she said, and she hopped out of the car.

There. There it is. A healthy amount of nerves, but enough courage to overcome.

That's just what Mother Pig told her boys. "Be careful of the Big Bad Wolf," she called as she waved goodbye.

Interpretation? Use your head, keep your wits about you, but have fun storming the castle.

✴ THE NO PHONE ZONE

But also for this very reason, giving all diligence, add to your faith,
virtue; and to virtue knowledge; and to knowledge, self-control;
and to self-control, perseverance; and to perseverance, godliness;
and to godliness, brotherly kindness; and to brotherly kindness,
love. For if these things are yours and abound, you will be neither
barren nor unfruitful in the knowledge of our Lord Jesus Christ.
For he who lacks these things is shortsighted, even to blindness,
and has forgotten that he was cleansed from his old sins.

2 PETER 1:5-9

Many, many years ago when my oldest two children were little, we lived at the edge of a cotton field outside of Memphis. We had two kids, one car, and few neighbors. Almost every day I would take the kids on the three-quarters of a mile walk down the gravel road to the mailbox in hopes of hearing from the latest editor to whom I had sent a submission.

Life was simple. Because we had no car during my husband's work hours, there was nowhere to go, and with our very limited budget, there was nothing to buy. As Bethany and Tiger put it, they had a cotton field and a mud puddle.

Fast forward eight more kids and thirty years. We had two cars, Internet, cable, iPods, iPhones, an XBox, and a PS4. (Have you gotten your iPhone yet? Could you tell me where the self-control app is located?)

I didn't want my kids to remember me always looking at my phone while they were talking to me. I was determined to be more intentional about it. Here are my on purpose, No Phone Zones:

- Mornings before school
- Afternoons after school
- Any time the family is hanging out
- Dinner time and just before bed

While I'm at it, let me toss in some boundaries for gaming. Though I was never completely happy with the amount of time my boys spent playing video games, these few rules seemed to make the difference between addiction and self-control.

- No games before lunch
- No more than an hour to an hour and a half a day
- Skip games completely twice a week in the summer
- No games at all Monday through Thursday during the school year
- No graphically violent games until they are older (depends on the kid, but somewhere around thirteen)

In her book, *It's Always Something*, the late Gilda Radner told a story about her cousin's dog who got tangled up with a lawn mower and lost her hind legs. The dog was expecting a litter of puppies, Radner wrote, and they thought for sure she would have to be put down. But surprisingly the vet said no, the puppies were fine; she could deliver them.

The dog eventually learned to walk without hind legs: *step, step, scoot; step, step, scoot.* The time came; she delivered the puppies. She nursed them and weaned them. When they learned to walk, they all walked like their mother: *step, step, scoot; step, step, scoot.*

No, there's no self-control app on that screen, only inside of me. If my kids were going to learn social media boundaries, it had to start with me. For just like those puppies, we all know that kids grow up not to do what we say but to do what we do.

✦ THE BENEFITS OF BOREDOM

*Flee also youthful lusts; but pursue righteousness, faith,
love, peace with those who call on the Lord out of a pure
heart. Avoid foolish and ignorant disputes, knowing that
they generate strife. And a servant of the Lord must not
quarrel but be gentle to all, able to teach, patient.*

2 TIMOTHY 2:22-24

I have always loved summer. A time for staying up, sleeping in, swimming, cookouts— also the perfect time for regularly inflicting boredom on kids.

If you asked my kids how I did this when we had a full house, they would recite my list: No screens of any kind before lunch. On Tuesdays and Thursdays no electronic games at all. Zip. None. Nada. A short list of daily chores and thirty minutes of reading, and there you have it: summer at the Sims' home.

When Cory was still in elementary school, he frequently called it torture. But my constant refrain was this: Summer isn't what it used to be.

When I was a kid, I would regularly hop on my bike with my lunch packed and go meet my BFF for a day of exploring. Be home by dinner was my mother's only rule. Most kids nowadays have no such luxury, as allowing long, unsupervised hours is simply too risky. Consequently, summer days call for structure, but leave plenty of time open for boredom.

Why welcome boredom? Because life is boring sometimes, and kids better be able to figure it out. It doesn't take too long for a mother to learn that to constantly entertain kids is exhausting and expensive, not to mention unfair to them.

Yes, like you, I dealt with boredom and bickering (they go hand in hand, don't they?). But I usually unearthed a neglected book or a board game, or threatened extra chores if they didn't find a way. It is interesting, though, that even when I didn't make a suggestion (or a threat), they eventually found the fun. For instance, Emma frequently pretended with or read to younger sister Dorothy, and Cory would sometimes get so creative as to make up a Star Wars movie with Silas, five years his junior.

I frequently reminded my kids that boredom is a blessing—it leaves you grateful for all the other times when you have something to do.

Our family spent a year in south Florida, living in the land of entertainment minutes from the beach and a few hours from Disney, Universal, and Legoland. Nothing wrong with these places that provide lots of fun (not to mention thousands of jobs), and we did visit a theme park or two before we left that part of the country. I am, after all, married to Captain Fun.

However, most days are ordinary, I remind my kids. Life is not Disney World. Life is life and Disney World is Disney World. We'd better make sure our kids know the difference.

 CHORE DAY

*In all labor there is profit, but idle
chatter leads only to poverty.*

PROVERBS 14:23

Around our house, Saturday was chore day, and complaining would get you way more than you bargained for.

"Okay, everybody," I'd announce with great enthusiasm each Saturday morning around 8:30. "Chores at 9:00."

"I hate Saturdays," at least one child always responded.

"Work is a blessing," I reminded them. "It means you have a full life, things to take care of, and people who need you."

But the collective moaning reminded me that hard work is something that almost always has to be taught to kids. They all bring different levels of work ethic to the table.

I recall one Saturday when we had leaves that needed to be raked and bagged—piles and piles of them. My husband was outside raking with our oldest son. Raking and bagging. For an hour they worked, with still so much more to go.

I could see through the sliding glass doors that the work session was unraveling. Tiger didn't want to finish, yet his dad was pushing him on. It tugged at this mother's heart. I opened the door, stuck my head out, and opened my mouth to intervene. His dad saw it coming and held his hand up. "Let me raise the man," he said. I guess even Captain Fun has to get serious sometimes.

I pulled my head back in and shut the door. Hard work was something each kid must learn, and it was a hard lesson. But when Tiger played

58

high school football, his coach said he had never, no never, coached such a hard-working kid. When he got his first job (and every one since), his boss bragged on what a hard worker he was. In fact, when he reached his early thirties, he called us to tell us that with his recent raise, his boss specifically mentioned his hard work and ability to take initiative.

Then there is our daughter, Mary, who specifically thanked us for teaching her how to work. As a student at the US Coast Guard Academy, she recalled summer training on the ship where she was required to do everything from scrubbing the deck to collecting and sorting the trash. "I'm so glad you made us do chores," she told me, "and especially grateful that Dad made us rake the leaves until we got it right. I already knew how to work hard when I got here."

Work is part of growing up, we tell our kids. Don't be afraid of it; embrace it, be intentional, take initiative. Hard work makes you stand out. While the younger ones moaned occasionally (they were still learning), we didn't let that stop us from teaching them how to work hard.

After all, parenting is the most important work of all. If you're intentional about it, you'll get more than you bargained for.

✳ THE WISDOM OF THE OOMPA LOOMPAS

For he who lacks these things is shortsighted, even to blindness and has forgotten that he was cleansed from his old sins. Therefore, brethren, be even more diligent to make your call and election sure, for if you do these things you will never stumble; for so an entrance will be supplied to you abundantly into the everlasting kingdom of our Lord and Saviour Jesus Christ.

2 PETER 1: 9-11

When Silas and Dorothy were ages nine and twelve, they made their Virginia debut at Broken Leg Theatre's production of Wonka, Jr. They were my little Oompa Loompas, and over the eight weeks of rehearsals, I concluded that the Oompa Loompa way of thinking is spot on. Each time those little lumpy creatures appeared on stage they offered a nugget of truth. My takeaway?

Concentrate on self-control (Augustus Gloop had zero) over self-esteem. Veruca Salt possessed plenty of that.

Make manners mandatory. The gum smacking, back talking Violet Beauregarde could've used a generous helping.

Instill gratitude. Veruca didn't get it and neither did her father. *Require* gratitude from your children. Encourage it when you can. Enforce it when you must.

Expect respect. Only Charlie Bucket, bless his heart, respected his elders. Enforce respect for your sake, for their sake, and for the good of the whole planet.

Perseverance—a.k.a., work ethic. Everybody needs one. It wouldn't hurt Veruca to get her hands dirty. Perhaps Augustus should have been required to work for food.

Limit screen time, even if they howl like Mike Teavee. While we're at it, we must set an example, unlike Mrs. Teavee, who was constantly on her own screen (in this production, at least).

I once interviewed author Kay Wyma, and she told me something that has stuck with me. "You know, I grew up privileged. Much of my young life consisted of tennis, laying poolside, and a brand new car when I turned sixteen, yet my father instilled two principles in me: the value of hard work and that I could do anything I set my mind to. He wasn't afraid to let me try and to let me fail."

That pretty much sums up the Oompa Loompa philosophy. Kids can't raise themselves. They need limits, guidance, discipline, nurturing. The one thing they don't need? For us to make their lives perfect.

If you have concluded that maybe your kid is a little too much like the kids who met their demise at Wonka's factory, try a little Oompa Loompa know-how. It's just good, common sense.

✦ THE PATH TO THE PEAK

*There are four things which are little on the earth, but they are
exceedingly wise: The ants are a people not strong, yet they prepare
their food in the summer; The rock badgers are a feeble folk, yet
they make their homes in the crags; The locusts have no king,
yet they all advance in ranks; The spider skillfully grasps with its
hands, and it is in kings' palaces.*

PROVERBS 30:24-28

"I wish I could make a speech at this ceremony and tell every kid who is not wearing cords and winning scholarships that they are doing just fine," my daughter Bethany said to me during yet another sibling's high school graduation.

She spoke from experience, as she, herself, admits that her grades were average during high school. No AP classes, no scholarships. Not. One. Cord. Yet Bethany had one thing that some of the cord bearers didn't have: she knew how to study, and it served her well.

After high school, she attended the University of Kentucky, graduating with a business degree. "But I didn't just walk right into my dream job, or my dream salary," she often reminded her younger siblings when they *oohed and ahhed* at her shiny life as a young professional in DC. She is also quick to confess that she even lost a job at one point and moved home for several months to sleep double on the bottom bunk.

But eventually, Bethany found her niche in marketing, then pursued her graduate degree from Georgetown in 2018. What's more, she was named Student of the Year in her program. "No one should peak in high school," she says, with conviction.

"Boy," her younger sister Mary said several months after her high school graduation (she was one of the ones winning the scholarships and wearing the cords), "you go through high school and finish in the top ten percent, you get all the cords and even a few medals, you win a full ride scholarship and even get named Student of the Year. Then you get to college and feel like an idiot."

Mary also spoke from experience. She did all of the above and was offered a scholarship to the United States Coast Guard Academy. The pressure was tremendous in this new atmosphere, and she admits she often felt like a buoy lost at sea. But time (and a lot of perseverance) changes everything. Mary learned a thing or two about herself: that she is no idiot, for one, and (though she would never say it, but since I'm her mother, I can) that she is an absolute beast both on the track and the rugby field. She even got an invitation to try out for USA Rugby, in fact. What's more, she entered her senior year as a Three Star Cadet, a title which recognizes high military, physical, and academic achievement. Her future looked brighter than ever.

Learning alongside some of the smartest kids in the country (even if you're one of them) at a school like the USCGA can be intimidating, but it still might be right where you belong. Sleeping on the bottom bunk with your seven-year-old sister can make you feel like a loser, even if it is exactly where you need to be.

I am so proud of these two girls. Their paths were not easy, yet they still found their way. How inspiring that they took very different approaches to the peak, yet reached the same conclusions:

The path to the peak looks different for everyone.

The journey is just as significant as the destination.

The growth cannot occur without the struggle.

Graduation season is a perfect time to encourage your kids that life is a process of growth and struggle, struggle and growth. Remind them to take a lesson from the ant, the badger, the locust and the spider: as long as they keep moving forward, they are doing just fine.

SECTION TWO:
FAITH

Mom Dot often says that faith is the very foundation of the Sims family. It's true. We can do everything else right, have all of our ducks (or kids) in a row, but as Hebrews 11 reminds us, without faith it is impossible to please Him.

HURRICANE ELVIS ✴

Therefore we do not lose heart. Even though our outward man is
perishing, yet the inward man is being renewed day by day. For
our light affliction, which is but for a moment, is working for us
a far more exceeding and eternal weight of glory, while we do not
look at the things which are seen, but at the things which are not
seen. For the things which are seen are temporary, but the things
which are not seen are eternal.

2 CORINTHIANS 4:16-18

Sitting with Kevlar on my windows while the last of Hurricane Gordon poured a steady rain had given me pause to reflect on the only hurricane Memphis ever had. If you're not from Memphis, you probably don't know about Hurricane Elvis, as I don't recall it making the national news. I remember it well, though, because Hurricane Elvis marked the beginning of one of the first real storms of our married life. I hope it encourages you in the midst of a trial.

On July 22, 2003, we were expecting our eighth baby. That afternoon was like any other July day; the air was still, the temperature was hot, and the kids were bored. Then the wind quietly, even eerily, stirred.

The sirens did not sound (when you grow up in Memphis, you grow accustomed to the tornado sirens), but the wind was not merely bending and snapping the trees, but sending them flying. Straight-line winds, we learned later; winds with the force of a tornado, only without the funnel cloud.

It was quick. It was quiet. The damage was extreme. The power was out and debris filled the yard. We all went out back, and as I waded through the broken branches, I saw the tiniest baby squirrel on the ground, umbilical cord still attached. For some reason, it made me think of my own baby. A sign, I would soon learn.

That night, in the middle of the night, I lost the baby at seven weeks along. It was my first miscarriage after having seven normal pregnancies that produced big, fat, overdue babies. Traumatic, to say the least.

Two days later, the power still out, we threw away all of the food in the fridge. For a family of nine, it was a small fortune.

On day three, the transmission on the car went out. *Cha-ching.*

On day four, some dear friends invited all nine of us to stay with them until our power was restored. I was so grateful to get a hot meal and a hot bath as, unbeknownst to the kids, I was still recovering from the loss of the baby. I love those folks; I will never forget their hospitality.

On day five (in our neighborhood, anyway) the power was restored. People were cheering the Memphis power workers in the streets.

With power on, we went home and restocked our fridge, only to realize by day seven that the fridge had gone kaput. For the second time, we threw away our food, and bought a new fridge. *Cha-ching.*

On day eight, the A/C joined the ranks of the transmission and the fridge. Kaput. Air conditioning in July in Memphis is not an option. *Cha-ching.*

To tie a bow around the whole thing, an opportunity to relocate fell through. In the span of eight days, we lost our baby, our savings, and our dream. The stress was unbelievable. It was the most pressure we had been under since we had been married. Hurricane Elvis left a mark I have never forgotten.

Fast forward one year. Baby Dorothy was twelve weeks old and we had just moved to Vermont. Our new friends had invited us to the annual Mozart Festival in Stowe. I was holding the baby while watching the sun sink behind the Green Mountains. As the sun was setting and Mozart was playing, it occurred to me it had been almost exactly a year since that terrible trial.

The revelation was shocking. If someone had told me during that awful week a year before, *Don't worry, in one year you will be sitting on a Vermont mountain top, watching the sunset, listening to Mozart while holding another new baby,* I would not have believed it.

The Captain and I learned a thing or two from those trying weeks: Trust in God and His goodness. Sometimes He works *in* us. Sometimes He works *on* us. Let trials pull you together, not apart.

That was many years ago, and whenever we face a new trial (and there is always one lurking, it seems) we point to that week and remind each other that God has always taken care of us. He is always working for our good.

I would not have chosen to go through the trials of that week so long ago, but I am thankful Hurricane Elvis came to visit us that day. I don't think we could have strengthened our faith any other way.

✳ TAKING THE LEAP

*But without faith it is impossible to please Him; for he
who comes to God must believe that He is, and that He
is a rewarder of those who diligently seek Him.*

HEBREWS 11:6

"I can't believe the way you will pack up your whole house, seven kids, two cats and a dog and just up and move from upstate New York to south Florida," Mom Dot said to me several times on our caravan (of which she was part) down to Florida.

She wasn't the only one.

"How scary," said a friend. "But how exciting," she quickly added.

"I'm jealous," said another friend.

My wonderful sisters—five of them, of which I am the baby—are always supportive, but I know they worry. "I am not sure I am capable of staying in one place too long," I told one of them. She agreed.

I wasn't born this way; it is something I have had to grow into. In fact, I used to be a timid soul when it came to taking chances. But then I married Robert the Risk Taker. Let's just say he rubbed off on me.

By risk I don't mean blindly leaping into the unknown. Well, not totally, anyway.

It all started when Captain Fun and I began to feel—what shall I call it?—the calling to leave the number of children we have up to God. I cannot explain it, but we both felt it. We were on the same page; both convinced that children are a blessing, a gift, a reward (Psalm 127). So we did. By the time number ten was on the way, I was 45 years old. There's not one of them I would send back.

Then my husband felt we were supposed to move from Memphis

to Vermont. *Can you do that?* I asked myself. The answer was yes. It changed our lives. It changed our children's lives, and all for the better, too.

After five wonderful years in Vermont, he left his place of employment and struck out on his own with a consulting business. I confess it was scary to me at the time, but I supported him, even though my knees were knocking. Opportunities have since taken us up and down the east coast. Often scary and uncertain, but oh, so exciting.

We do our homework when we take a risk. We research, we pray, we do the math. Then if doors open and God seems to be leading forward, we take the leap.

One of the saddest sights I have ever seen is people who do their homework: they measure, calculate, analyze, they pray and ask God for direction. But when it comes to taking the leap, they just can't, or won't, do it.

"Careful of waiting for everything to be perfect before you make a move," I exhorted my oldest daughter, reminding her of our big, beautiful (but never perfect) picture.

As I stop and reflect on our life together, I am so glad the Captain and I took the leap of having ten kids. That he had the courage to move and move again. So glad I submitted that first magazine article in hopes it would be published; addressed that first MOPS group so many years ago; attended that writer's conference *again* to submit my book proposal. If I hadn't taken these risks, I never would have known what could be.

I guess another word for risk taking is faith. It isn't reckless, but it is blind sometimes. It is almost always plain scary. But God meets it, honors it, blesses it. Every time.

Are you standing on the edge with your toes curled around the cliff? Have you prepared and prayed the best you know how? Ask God for direction. But be warned—He will give it.

When He does, be ready to take the leap.

✳ SHARKS AND SNAKES AND TOADS, OH MY!

*Therefore do not worry about tomorrow, for
tomorrow will worry about its own things.
Sufficient for the day is its own trouble.*

MATTHEW 6:34

I am not a worrier, a wimp, a glass-half-empty kind of mother. *Buck up, Figure it out,* and *Take initiative* are three of my favorite phrases to utter to my children. It's a tough world after all, and your kids better be ready for it when they leave the nest.

Captain Fun teases the kids that unless injuries involve blood or someone's head being on backwards, don't bother to tell Mom. No, I didn't worry that time three of my boys went flying with their oldest brother, Tiger. They could not have been in more capable hands.

During our year in Florida, however, I found myself skittish at the ocean. The locals told me you have more of a chance of being struck by lightning than being bitten by a

shark. But I had been keeping score: the shark attacks were the clear leader. What's more, a poor teen lost half his arm to an alligator at an area lake.

Though these terrible happenings were local, I still felt a bit distant from them. But then my next-door neighbor brought me a picture of a snake and a toad she found in her yard—a mere fifty feet from my own back door. "Show these to your kids," she said, "and warn them not to touch them." Both ugly beasts were not only poisonous but also deadly.

It, well, *scared* me.

From that day on, my morning walks with Hope got me thinking about all the predators, both human and animal, that could hurt my kids. All the accidents that could happen—things over which I had no control. These glass-half-empty thoughts continually crept into my mind, and I confess, it started to overwhelm me.

So how does a mother keep from panicking? I stay on my knees. Well, not really. But I go there daily to talk to my own parent and tell Him what's troubling me. I open His book and read His promises.

Then I trust. I trust that what happens has to pass through His hands first. I resolve that, come what may, life will make me better, not bitter.

 THERE IT IS

Unless the Lord builds the house, they labor in vain who build it.
Unless the Lord guards the city, the watchman stays awake in vain.

PSALM 127:1

Sitting in church one Sunday, I inspected our seats to see if eight of the ten kids had arrived. (Hope was in the nursery, and our oldest and his wife were still sparring with winter in frozen North Dakota.) One, two, three…six, seven, eight. My eyes followed to the end where my husband of 28 years finished off the row. Every single chair was occupied by a Sims.

Suddenly, I was struck with the wonder of it: There it is. What I have wanted since I was nine years old. I held my breath, my eyes misted. I wanted to stretch my arms all the way down that row and pull them all close.

From the time I was a child, I had desired a big family. After I committed my life to Christ at the age of nine, a big, Christian family became my vision, my quest.

There they were. Oldest daughter Bethany sitting between her two little brothers, both of whom attended West Point. Both towered over their big sister. Matt, who was newly engaged (we love her), and Ben settled in after singing "O Holy Night" to our adult Sunday school class, which touched me so deeply.

Mary and Emma, just seventeen months apart; both runners, so different, yet the best of friends. Cory, unassuming and a bit stoic, until he surprises you with his quick wit. Silas and Dorothy, happily chatting and drawing in their children's bulletins.

I couldn't know when I started all

that this calling would entail. Long days, longer nights. The mayhem, the mess, the mountains of laundry. The mountains of *money* (kudos to the Captain, our breadwinner). For brief moments the vision became blurred when both the Captain and I (and everyone else) questioned our sanity at having such a brood.

It wasn't until they began to grow up, to launch, that I started to understand where all this was going. "Like arrows in the hand of a warrior, so are the children of one's youth," Psalm 127:4 says. A strong family? It's like a weapon that equips us to fight life's battles.

And here we were, worshiping together in a full pew with full hearts, and full of wonder this Christmas Eve at the miracle of it all. Ten kids, a happy family. Not without struggle or flaws or fears, but still steady, connected, grateful.

I say to myself, "There it is," and I know we exist only because of His strength, His mercy, His grace and for His glory.

✳ ALL THE DIFFERENCE

*Then little children were brought to Him that He might put His
hands on them and pray, but the disciples rebuked them. But Jesus
said, 'Let the little children come to Me, and do not forbid them;
for of such is the kingdom of heaven.' And He laid His hands on
them and departed from there.*

MATTHEW 19:13-15

When Silas had four good days in a row at preschool one week, I told him how proud I was. As we pulled away from the school that day, his response surprised me. "Jesus took all the badness away and put in His goodness."

That night, his words were confirmed by Captain Fun when we got home. Silas wanted to pray a few nights before, he said, to trust Christ as his Savior. Perhaps he heard something that stirred him at church, or maybe at home during family devotions that Robert is so faithful about leading every night. Whatever the reason, it was on his mind and he spoke up and said he was ready. So his dad led Silas in what I grew up knowing as the sinner's prayer.

When I was a younger mom I might have thought, "Whoa, now, wait a minute, he cannot possibly understand at barely five years old." But now I tend to step out of the way and let Jesus do His work. Don't forbid the children to come, He reminds us in Matthew.

The Lord did His part. Silas did his part. I had to do my part. It is where the little word faith comes in.

But aren't people generally good? Do we really need forgiveness, repentance, change, redemption? I believe we do, as I refer to where Paul writes in Galatians 2:21 "...if righteousness can be obtained by the law, then Christ died for nothing."

Because I believe the words of

Jesus, I teach them to my children. When they respond, I let them.

Of course I encountered more of Silas's mischief, but I also saw such change in that little boy. That's what Jesus does—as someone so eloquently put it—He changes our "want to."

That makes all the difference.

✴ A GOOD SHOT

Finally, my brethren, be strong in the Lord and in the power of His might. Put on the whole armor of God, that you may be able to stand against the wiles of the devil. For we do not wrestle against flesh and blood, but against principalities, against powers, against the rulers of the darkness of this age, against spiritual hosts of wickedness in the heavenly places. Therefore take up the whole armor of God, that you may be able to withstand in the evil day, and having done all, to stand.

EPHESIANS 6: 10-13

"**M**om," Silas said one day when he came home from school, "there is a mean kid in my class, and I'm trying to hold up my shield of faith, but he sure is a good shot."

What a simple reminder to make sure I put on my own armor every day. After all, if my seven-year-old second grader had the presence of mind to be thinking in the spirit realm when someone was unkind, so should I.

"Put on the whole armor of God," the apostle Paul admonishes in Ephesians chapter 6, "that you may be able to stand against the wiles of the devil." He goes on to say that the real battle isn't with people; we are really fighting against principalities, powers, rulers of darkness and spiritual forces of wickedness in heavenly places.

There's a list to make a mother worry.

But, thank the Lord, there is more. The good news is he spends the next four verses on another list, a specific list of the armor with which God equips us to fight the battle:

- The belt of truth
- The breastplate of righteousness
- Feet covered with the Gospel of peace
- Shield of faith ("Above all else," Paul writes, "it is faith that will help you quench all the fiery

78

darts of the wicked one.")

- The helmet of salvation
- The sword of the Spirit (the Word, he tells us)

Pray, watch, persevere, Paul concludes. Sounds like a battle to me.

"It worked!" Silas told his dad the next day as he bursts through the door. "I held up my shield of faith and it worked!" At first, he told me, he ignored the kid. Now they were friends.

The mama bear in me wanted to fight his battles for him—call the teacher, call the mother, call the kid. But I know my bigger job is usually to step out of the way and allow God to build those spiritual muscles. After all, this was practice for life's bigger battles. This time it was the kid on the playground; next time it would be the college roommate or coworker.

All this talk of spiritual warfare made me realize that I too often failed to remind my kids before they headed out the door: Put on your armor—all of it.

Because just like Silas so articulately said, there is always somebody, somewhere who is a good shot.

✦ FINDING A SYSTEM

How sweet are Your words to my taste, Sweeter than honey to my mouth! Through Your precepts I get understanding; Therefore, I hate every false way. Your word is a lamp to my feet and a light to my path.

PSALM 119:103-105

As a mother, I am forever trying to find a system that works. Exploring more efficient ways to run things can really change your life.

Take television, for example. Years ago, my kids were watching TV every day after school for two hours or more. Then they began on their homework, bleary eyed and foggy brained. It was my sister who passed along her rule of no screens on school nights. Implementing that system tightened up our daily routine, and on Fridays they all looked forward to the screens of their choice.

Getting the dishes done was another area that was sinking me. The bigger our family got, the longer the dishes took. When washing dishes till after 7:00 was becoming routine, I enlisted the kids to help. First I tried announcing, "When it is your night to say the blessing, it is your night to help with the dishes." Captain Fun nixed it though, wanting the kids to look forward to saying grace instead of associating it with their turn to wash dishes. Fair enough. That's why I call him Captain Fun.

Then I tried to assign the dishes according to birth order. Child number one would wash dishes on Monday, the second born on Tuesday, and so forth. But when you have more kids than days of the week, that won't work either. Even I can do that math.

When I got down to six kids

at home, I finally figured out the simple system of alternating boys night/girls night. With three of each left at home, it was fast and fair.

But the one system I found that changed my life more than anything else was tweaking my morning routine. Most mornings, I got up about an hour before the kids—when they were all sleeping all night—for my quiet time. I made the coffee first thing, prayed while it was brewing, poured myself a cup, and read a passage. Did you know there are thirty-one chapters in Proverbs and thirty-one days in most months? Divine wisdom throughout that book.

Prayer and Bible reading has been my lifeline since I was just a kid. Psalm 119:105 says, "Your word is a lamp unto my feet and a light unto my path."

A lamp and a light. You won't find anything more life changing than that.

 WHEN GOD WORKS

*A man's heart plans his way, but
the Lord directs his steps.*
PROVERBS 16: 9

A few months after we moved from Florida to Virginia, the Captain was driving around, praying he could buy me a house (*love that man*). He felt a nudge to turn down a certain street into a certain neighborhood. He knew at once the houses were just my taste: older homes with a little space around them and lots of trees. "Lord," he prayed as he parked at the end of a cove, "please let me buy a house like one of these for Margie."

He spotted a certain yellow house—he was parked in front of it, in fact. He thought he felt a nudge to go knock on that bright red door and ask if they wanted to sell their house. Nah.

We talked on and off about buying a house, but we thought it would be smart to launch a few more kids, buy a smaller house and save several thousand dollars—there *is* a big price difference between a six bedroom home and a four bedroom home.

Spring came and our landlord said he wanted to sell the house we were renting. Were we interested? But the house we were renting was too much house even for us: seven bedrooms with too much kitchen for someone who doesn't like to cook (though I do it anyway). An open floor plan that was far too noisy for a house where eleven people resided.

We started looking for another house to rent. Then the Captain suggested maybe we shouldn't rule

82

out buying. He found a realtor and told me to look on her website and see what I thought. I liked that she mentioned the importance of family on her home page, so we gave her a call.

Robert gave her a list of what he wanted, not really thinking such a house was on the market at that time: six bedrooms, a mother-in-law wing, an acre of land, and *maybe* a stream. She showed us three houses that at least had some things on the list. We loved the second one, but by the time we decided to make an offer, it was gone. "You know," she said at the end of the day, "my parents have been talking about selling their house for over a year and it sounds like just what you want. Would you like for me to call my dad so you can see it?"

We said yes.

Nine of the ten kids were home that day. The older three had gone to dinner and said they would meet us there. Mom Dot stayed with Hope, who had already gone to bed. The Captain and I loaded up the other six and drove over. (Like I said, when we move, it is a complex operation.) "Sometimes God is working when you don't even know it," I said on the way over.

We typed the address into the GPS and it led us right into the driveway of the yellow house with the red door. "This is the house," said the Captain, and told us the story.

The realtor's dad was watching the grandkids, but her mom greeted us with a smile, and by the time six kids poured through her front door, she was beaming. "You have a beautiful family," she said.

"You have a beautiful house," we answered.

About the time we got to the back yard (complete with stream) the other three kids came around the side. She shook her head and tears filled her eyes. (Really, it's true—and she hadn't even seen Hope's cheeks yet). "Look at this family. Look at this beautiful family."

We followed her into the den. "Sometimes God is working and we don't even know it," she said.

"That's what *I* just said," I told her.

"We would love to buy your house," the Captain said.

"I would love for you to buy my house." More tears.

"You look like you need a hug," said the Captain. Group hug; then, as he is known to do, the Captain said a prayer. Right there. In the middle of that den.

On closing day, we stopped by the house to finalize furniture and bedroom placement (remember, complex operation). We found two pounds of coffee on the table with a note. *Welcome to this house of healing and peace. May you have many years of happiness here.*

Life can be complicated. We struggle and strain. We doubt. We try to figure it out. But God is working. And when God works, you might not see it at first.

But when He finally points the way, you just can't miss it.

PROMS AND PRAYERS

*And let us not grow weary while doing good, for in
due season we shall reap if we do not lose heart.*
GALATIANS 6:9

We were sitting around the dinner table one evening when it dawned on me—it was that time of year again.

"Ben, isn't prom coming up soon?"

"Saturday night," he said, gulping down another bite of Pioneer Woman's Sour Cream Noodle Bake. (Love that stuff.)

"Aren't you going?" asked Captain Fun. Not a surprising question coming from the Captain.

"Wasn't planning on it."

The Fun in Captain Fun took over. "You should go, Ben. It is your senior prom."

"You're going to regret it," I said. "I didn't go to my prom, and I regret it." I know about these things,

even though my nickname lacks the word fun.

Ben explained himself. "I wasn't even going to mention it after the car and the choir trip expenses."

Ben had put a ping in the twelve-passenger van a few weeks before. Okay, a little more than a ping. Call it a mega-ping to the tune of $2,000.

"I want to buy you a ticket, Ben," insisted the Captain. The conversation lingered over dinner, the other siblings chimed—or clamored—in. (The Sims kids have been known to raise their hands at the dinner table when deemed necessary.)

Mom Dot chimed in, too. "I want to see you in that tux with that high voltage smile of yours."

The Captain talked him into it. I

wrote the check, but Ben left it sitting on the counter the next day. Time was short, but he vowed he would buy a ticket.

That night while we were in the midst of March Madness, the doorbell rang. No one was there. I confess I blamed Silas. One of his pranks, I thought. (Sorry, Silas.)

Then Dorothy noticed something. An envelope. Taped to the door. With BEN SIMS written on it. Ben wasn't home. We *oohed* and *aahed*. Mom Dot held it up to the light, then shook it and said steam might do the trick. She then suggested opening it in a way that looked like an accident.

When Ben got home from work the kids mobbed him, smashing the envelope into his hand. He opened it with an audience—there's always an audience at our house. $200 tumbled out. Ben read the anonymous note:

Dear Ben,

Your love of God and people are refreshing in this day and age. It has come to our attention that you may not be attending your prom. Please use this money for prom (or however else you may see fit).

Psalm 37:4

Ben was touched. I don't think he would mind my telling that he even got a little teary. "What a witness you are, Ben," I said.

But there was even more to it than that, and I knew it. This, like so many other things that happened during his final year of high school, was an answer to a mother's prayer.

I know you moms understand the sort of prayer I'm talking about. The kind of prayer that you pray when friendships are slow to form, when not everyone is nice, when things get hard. When your kid goes to three different high schools in four years, you worry a little and you pray a lot.

So, I started praying somewhere along the middle of his junior year, *Lord, please take care of Ben. Give him a fun senior year. He is such a people person, Lord, just send him some fun.*

That September he got voted onto the homecoming court, and the following spring he was voted Most Outgoing of the senior class. Then someone anonymously paid his way to prom and wrote him a note he will never forget. What's more, he was crowned Prom King of the prom he almost missed.

"Be anxious for nothing," Philippians 4:6 tells us, "but in everything by prayer and supplication with thanksgiving let your requests be made known unto God."

Pray for, with, and about your

kids. When they are little, when they are teenagers, when they are grown. Pray about the big things. Pray about the little things. Pray about everything. That's what it says. Everything.

Even the prom.

✴ SOMETHING'S COMING

*Ask, and it will be given to you; seek, and you will find; knock,
and it will be opened to you. For everyone who asks receives,
and he who seeks finds, and to him who knocks, it will be
opened. Or what man is there among you who, if his son asks
for bread, will give him a stone? Or if he asks for a fish, will he
give him a serpent? If you then, being evil, know how to give
good gifts to your children, how much more will your Father
who is in heaven give good things to those who ask Him!*

MATTHEW 7:7-11

*I*t was that time of year again: launch time. Our fourth one was preparing for takeoff.

An important looking package had come in the mail a few months earlier. Mom Dot, the official mail-checker of the house, trotted in with it tucked under her arm. It had Ben's name on it.

We had been waiting to hear what the next step was for our soon to be graduating son. Ben had applied to several colleges and two of the academies. So far, he had received one acceptance to a local university and had been wait listed by others. But his senior year was clicking on by, and we were getting a little anxious.

As the family gathered around him that afternoon, the thought crossed my mind that when only an envelope arrives from a college or academy, it is usually a no. However, this was a BFE (Big Fat Envelope), a thick Priority Mail package from the USMA Prep School in West Point, New York.

We know the Prep School well, as (by God's grace) we already had one son attend there. Matthew was a prepster and went on to attend West Point. We are both proud and grateful.

Ben tore the package open to reveal a leather-bound folder with United States Military Academy Prep School imprinted on the front. An appointment. We screamed. We jumped. We high-fived. We celebrated.

Because we felt the deadline had passed, I had stopped praying about the Prep School. His dad had stopped praying. Ben had stopped praying. But not Mom Dot. She never gave up. She never quit asking.

Ben called his brother Matt to tell him the news. He already knew. In fact, he had known for three days.

"Isn't that just like the Lord?" older sister, Bethany, said. "Something is always coming."

Excuse me while I go look in the mirror and have a talk with myself that goes something like this: Oh, ye of little faith.

We pray. We worry. We grow weary. We stop praying. But God is working. God is listening. God is already answering.

Even when we can't see it, something is always coming.

✦ THE GOODNESS OF GOD

*Now to Him who is able to do exceedingly abundantly
above all that we ask or think, according to the power
that works in us, to Him be glory in the church by Christ
Jesus to all generations, forever and ever. Amen.*

EPHESIANS 3:20-21

Ben's graduation from West Point Prep School (USMAPS) was quickly approaching, and we were making plans for the trip. Being the practical mom that I am, I was inclined to hop in the car with the Captain for a simple trip where just the two of us ran up to attend the festivities and bring him home. But, as his nickname implies, Captain Fun wanted to take the crew along. (Family fun would be scarce without him, I know.)

We took all who were available and could afford to miss a few days of school—the four youngest kids and Grandma. (Mom Dot, by the way, is part of that Greatest Generation, and was busting her buttons over having two grandsons at West Point.)

Once we finally got in the car, I was always glad we brought the kids, grateful they would have the memory of this amazing place. Every American needs to experience the USMA. Honestly, like nowhere else I've visited, the campus of West Point kind of puts me in a trance.

It. Is. Awesome.

I have been pondering exactly why it affects me this way. Maybe it is the history, maybe it's the stoic, gray halls themselves. ("Is this a castle?" Hope kept asking.)

Maybe it's the Hudson that flows steadily, dependably alongside the campus. Perhaps the pomp and circumstance that accompanies any West Point ceremony. The ball, for instance, that preempted the dinner was grand. What's more, Ben said the invocation as his brother had done four years ago. It warms a mother's heart.

LTG (R) Thomas F. Metz ('71) delivered what I believe was the best live speech I have ever heard. The entire speech was captivating, but his last point has stuck with me:

Scan. Focus. Act.

He was addressing future soldiers, of course, but he did exhort the rest of us that these three words were applicable in any circumstance, any line of work.

Indeed. As moms, it summed up what we do every day. It put a name to it, which somehow energized me for the remaining mission ahead—a mission I had already been on for years, yet a mission I knew I would continue indefinitely.

No matter the reason I go—"A" Day, "R" Day, Parent Weekend, or graduation—West Point always moves me. The flags wave, the music plays, I grow nostalgic and wish I could call my parents and have a lengthy conversation about them having two grandsons at West Point. I know they, too, would bust their buttons.

Then it comes like a flood—the inspiration. The moment I remember that it is all from God's hand, simply because of His goodness in hearing the prayer of a nine-year-old girl (that was me) who wanted to have "a bunch of kids and a Christian family."

Even before I was half way through this parenting journey, He had already done "more than I could ask or think," just like Ephesians 3:20 promises. As my good friend in New York used to say, it's all God.

All because of His goodness. All for His glory.

 PASSAGES

Oh, taste and see that the Lord is good; blessed is the man who trusts in Him! Oh, fear the Lord, you His saints! There is no want to those who fear Him. The young lions lack and suffer hunger, but those who seek the Lord shall not lack any good thing.

PSALM 34:8-10

It had been a summer of passages, and I was trying to wrap my mind (and heart) around it. I had attempted to write about each separate summer passage, but words escaped me (a rare occurrence). Finally, on the official last day of summer 2015, I took one more stab at wrapping all of summer's events into one story.

Not long after school dismissed, my kids began visiting their brother Tiger (who gets the Oldest Brother Award). First Matt visited, then Ben went to see him. Finally, Mary and Emma took the train to sister Bethany (who is up for Oldest Sister Award), and the three of them visited Tiger for a long weekend. You young moms will understand—you know how you dream when they all grow up, you hope they like each other? That time was upon me, and they did!

Summer was rolling along, when I had a realization: It was the first summer in twenty-eight years that I hadn't had to wake up at the crack of dawn with a baby or toddler. For almost three decades I'd set my alarm for 5:30, only to have the latest baby wake up at 5:15. It had been a long twenty-seven years.

But that summer? That summer I had been sleeping until 6:20 and no one (except my athletes) stirred until 7:30. Do you know that seventy minutes is ample time for prayer, two cups of coffee, a scripture reading and a nice, long chat with my husband? Whew, just in the nick of time.

Captain Fun and I were filled with joy over our two parent visits to West Point that August. Once for Ben's "A" Day, where the new cadets get accepted after completing Basic Training, also known as BEAST. West Point is a fortress, with tall, gray stone buildings silently standing guard along the Hudson River. I cannot describe the emotions I felt as the band played and about three thousand upperclassmen marched out of each building in unison and lined up facing the incoming class of cadets, who numbered around nine hundred.

After some introductions and pageantry, all grew silent, and a commanding voice came over the speaker. "Class of 2019, welcome to the United States Military Academy." The new cadets, now earning the title of Plebes, marched toward their fellow cadets, turning to join their ranks. The tipping point for me, though, was having a son in both groups. Matthew, my Firstie, as the seniors were called, was welcoming Ben, the Plebe. What is a mother to do with all that emotion?

Two weeks later was Matthew's Ring Weekend, complete with ceremony and "hop," as it's called, which Matt's lovely fiancé, Melissa, was able to attend. Seniors received their class rings, and Mom a match-ing pendant. I still cannot find the words to describe the joy of dancing with one West Point cadet son, only to have another West Point cadet son cut in. Cinderella's got nothing on me.

I'm not ashamed to say that I had the big Five-O passage that summer. Call me crazy, but I didn't mind turning fifty. Mom Dot had been telling me for years that your fifties are younger than your forties, and I had anticipated being an "older woman who teaches the younger women," as described in Titus chapter two. It's a turbulent time to raise kids on this planet. Warts and all, I am eager to share.

My five older sisters summoned me to Cincinnati for a Baby Birthday weekend. There was a present by the coffee pot when I went to pour my coffee, and another on the bathroom sink when I went to brush my teeth. Later that day was a Reds game, filet-mignon on the grill, reminiscing about our parents, and presents, presents, presents.

The first morning we were together, I was the last one up. When I came into the room, all of my sisters were already sipping coffee. They all stopped to greet me, "Hey, Baby! Good morning." It sounded just like the greeting my own kids gave our baby, Hope, when she entered the room, and I had to laugh. No passage on being the baby, and that's okay with me.

And you better believe Captain Fun celebrated as only he can do by taking me back up to West Point for the Army football season opener. Seven of the ten kids were there (Mary and Emma graciously offered to stay back with Mom Dot, and my oldest was saving his time for Christmas). I love West Point. I love football. I got to see my two cadets at the game. What could be better? The Captain's conclusion was correct; it was a magical weekend. I thanked him from the bottom of my heart.

As that memorable summer came to an end, I eagerly anticipated the new school year, no doubt filled with passages of its own. So much behind me, yet so much ahead.

I'm still learning: submit it, surrender it, and embrace it all.

JUST RIGHT ✦

*Every good gift and every perfect gift is from above
and comes down from the Father of Lights with
whom there is no variation or shadow of turning.*

JAMES 1:17

The year flew by, several of my daughters confirmed one Thanksgiving morning as we cooked together.

After dinner was in the books, and the dishes were in the dishwasher (thanks to the men of the family, as it's what they do after the women cook all morning), I was thinking in list form—perhaps because of the pressing feeling to get my shopping done (but don't worry, I am not a T-Day shopper).

I did, however, make a Thanksgiving list that can be broken down into three parts, kind of like in Goldilocks: Too Much. Not Enough. Just Right.

Too Much

Food: Enough said.

Blessing: Captain Fun and I could hardly contain it.

Fun: Everyone pitched in here, but the Captain himself owned this one, starting with the annual Thanksgiving Day football game.

Cuteness: Hope owns this one, we all agreed.

Noise: But it was happy noise so it's all good.

Not Enough

Time: Hate to be redundant, but it flies.

Kids, believe it or not: My first born was missing, along with my first daughter-in-law. Love those two.

Room: See below. I think this challenge will only get more complicated. Emma says, in fact, that they are all having ten kids so that we will have 100 grandchildren. Bring it on.

Hot water: With twelve in the house, I could tell the hot water was iffy so a few times I skipped washing my hair.

Towels: Washer and dryer were running constantly.

Just Right

The weather: 64 and sunny. Thank you, Heavenly Father.

The turkey: Our generous new neighbor, himself a father of eight, offered to smoke it. We accepted.

Reflection: As is our tradition, each one took a turn sharing what made them thankful. After we re-membered and had a good laugh at Cory's quote when he was three (candy and money), we all got pretty serious about naming gratitude. It's always touched me, as this was exactly the kind of moment I pictured in my mind when I was a girl who someday wanted a lot of kids.

Gratitude: I was thinking about how much love is in our family. My older kids went to see each other. On purpose. The younger ones always squealed in delight when they came home.

Love and Gratitude—they go hand in hand. And when love and gratitude go together, they make everything just right.

THE TALENT SHOW

He shall be like a tree planted by the rivers of water, that
brings forth its fruit in its season, whose leaf also shall
not wither; and whatever he does shall prosper.

PSALM 1:3

I f I ever meet a lonely Christmas, I suspect I will have to find the nearest throng and join in. Being the youngest of eight, my Christmas traditions were always packed with people. As the mother of ten, the holidays still call for a crowd.

Though I have never been alone at Christmas, there have been seasons when everything changes. Whether parents age or families relocate, the time eventually comes for new traditions, and the transition can be emotional and draining. It was during one of these times of adjustment, however, that we found a tradition that has endured.

When we left a lifetime in Memphis to relocate to Vermont, friendships formed instantly. I was unsure of what those Vermonters would think of our big southern family, but they quickly embraced us, even calling our southern twang charming. A Christmas Eve open house seemed like the obvious answer to the search for a new tradition. Our church held Christmas Eve services, after all, and folks could come eat before or after church. A new tradition was born, with a Vermont white Christmas almost guaranteed, to boot.

In the five years we lived in Vermont, we only missed one year of the Christmas Eve Open House. My father had passed away in November and I was expecting another baby. I didn't feel up to it, as it was one of those transitional seasons of grief and change. A new tradition was needed, and the Christmas Eve Family Talent Show was born.

The talent show happens right after our traditional holiday menu of ham on Christmas Eve (followed by my grandfather's bean soup on Christmas Day). The Christmas Eve spread is always formal. We crowd around the table, join hands, say grace and savor the moment. Then the talent show begins.

First up is usually Mom Dot's lengthy passage from Macbeth (which she could still quote at nearly ninety). Her hands slicing through the air, the emotion in her voice, was always a sight to behold—compelling, convincing, poignant. Then, finally, upon exiting the stage, she turns and declares, "I don't believe a word of that." While I am glad she is more optimistic than Shakespeare, I love the fact that Grandma's recital will be etched in the minds of my children.

Every year, Silas dons a white lab coat and oversized glasses, setting up a makeshift lab in front of the fireplace. He was seven when we first introduced the Talent Show. That first year, he scurried around his laboratory, then looked up and gasped. "Oh, hello! I didn't see you there." He pressed his glasses higher on his nose. "My name is Dr. Silas Sims, and today we will be conducting a science experiment." He then proceeded to mix baking soda and vinegar and got the expected result—and some unexpected applause.

Cory's first act, at age thirteen, was demonstrating the art of speed-eating chocolate bars. Ten-year-old sister Dorothy followed with a gymnastics/dance routine. More applause.

Mary and Emma, then fifteen and seventeen, performed "Sisters" from the movie *White Christmas*, using branches from our tree trimming as their feathery fans.

Matt and Ben, both feeling liberated by their break from West Point, broke out the musical instruments and inspired us with worship songs.

One year, as a spontaneous surprise (even to him), my husband and I did a rendition of "I've Got You, Babe," karaoke style. The kids howled, secretly filming it. (And it shall forever remain a secret).

Daughter Bethany always concludes with "O Holy Night," a cappella. Everyone sits silently, as it is the most sacred time of our Christmas Eve, the only exception being the reading of the Christmas story around the tree.

We never know when we will all be together for Christmas, but on the occasion that my married kids call to tell us they are coming, I tell them to get their acts ready.

While we gave up the Christmas Eve Open House many years ago, the talent show has remained, even grown. No matter where we live, I want my kids to remember this tradition like a record stuck on repeat, marked in their memories until they are celebrating Christmas with their children.

We have seen many Christmas celebrations come and go in our years together. As much as I would love to still be heading to my mom's house on Christmas day, I have learned that life is seasonal; we must lean into the changes. After all, no matter where we live or what is under the tree, the one thing that matters most is that we celebrate together.

✴ THE PERFECT CHRISTMAS

*For unto us a child is born, unto us a Son is given, and the
government will be upon His shoulder. And His name will
be called Wonderful, Counselor, Mighty God, Everlasting
Father, Prince of Peace. Of the increase of His government
and peace there will be no end, upon the throne of David
and over His kingdom, to order it and establish it with
judgment and justice from that time forward, even forever.
The zeal of the Lord of hosts will perform this.*

ISAIAH 9:6-7

The older I get, the faster Christmas comes. If I'm not careful, it can turn into an annual race to see if I can get my gift and grocery shopping done before the December 24th deadline.

I have learned to let go, though. To lower my own expectations and encourage my children to lower theirs. After all, creating the perfect Christmas is tricky.

For instance, I relish the ritual of mailing almost a hundred Christmas cards every year. The year I had a December baby due, I mailed seven, photo not included. Some of the cards I received lay in a pile instead of hanging on my front door—a tradition my mother held that I have carried on, keeping her close.

Some years I don't get everything on the kids' lists. In fact, I had to whisper in Silas' ear one Christmas morning before the present rush that there was not one bucket of military men available in the whole county. What's more, that same year I couldn't find the right size boots for Mary and I forgot to get an extra-large bag of Craisins for Emma's stocking.

I can blame any imperfect Christmas on having ten children—that excuse is good for a lot of things. One year, I blamed the toothache that sent me to the dentist the day before Christmas Eve—there was a root canal in my future (though it happened to be the same year we had canceled the open house and that was a happy coincidence).

But if it weren't for the above reasons, it would be something else. Truth is, I have yet to find the perfect Christmas.

The year my mother died, that Christmasy feeling seemed to elude me, and each time Faith Hill's "Where Are You, Christmas?" came on the radio, I had to make a quick exit. Some seasons are like that.

But I have found the little things can also sabotage the perfect Christmas, if you let them. We moms can really get irritated over not having the perfect table, immaculate house, or just the right gift. We can always find something to fret about.

Christmas is first, of course, a celebration centered on the birth of the Savior followed by the traditions that steep us in the season. At the Sims' house that means ham on Christmas Eve and bean soup on Christmas day, pajama clad kids for 24 hours, oldest daughter Bethany singing "O Holy Night" on Christmas Eve, and no present rush until at least 6:00 A.M.

The traditions continue, with new ones born every year. Through the years, I have learned that Christmas doesn't have to be perfect, just embraced.

Imperfections and all.

✸ THE WONDER OF IT ALL

He who is faithful in what is least is faithful also in much; and he who is unjust in what is least is unjust also in much. Therefore, if you have not been faithful in the unrighteous mammon, who will commit to your trust the true riches? And if you have not been faithful in what is another man's, who will give you what is your own?

LUKE 16:10-12

So much had been simmering at our house the spring of 2016, it was boiling (and I was bubbling) over. My heart was so full.

For four years (plus a year at the Prep School) our son had been on a journey to graduate from West Point. It was a goal he'd had since he was about seven, when he told his dad he wanted to be a soldier. I had never even heard of the place, but the Captain put the dream in Matt's heart. "If you want to be a soldier, you should go to West Point."

Upon graduating, he became Second Lt. Matthew Sims, United States Army. Just a week later, we headed back to New York and were delighted to welcome a new addition to our family as (after an eighteen-month engagement) he married his fiancé, Melissa.

Two weeks after his wedding, our daughter Mary graduated from high school. Seventeen days later she reported to the Coast Guard Academy. What a banner senior year she had, getting into both West Point and The Coast Guard Academy, up for Scholar Athlete in our county (complete with photo in the newspaper), receiving recognition from her teachers with outstanding student awards. Most important, she was described by her teachers as one who "approaches everyone she meets with kindness and compassion." The best part of watching it all unfold was Mary's own amazement, shock, surprise that the honors were really hers.

I kept thinking about the wonder of it all.

The reigning Vice President spoke at West Point's graduation. A relaxed speaker who addressed the cadets more like an army buddy than the Vice President of the United States, Biden laughed a lot and cursed a lot. He admonished the newest army officers that they would get the job done. For the most part, an inspiring speech, and what an honor to hear a sitting Vice President in person.

Hats were tossed and children scurried across the field to find notes and money the cadets had tucked inside for them, a tradition at all the academies. It is unanimous among cadets, it seems, that they never want to see that West Point uniform again. When Matt asked if I wanted his, I immediately said *yes*. It is hanging in my closet, awaiting his younger brother Ben's uniform to hang alongside it in a few more years.

When I was a young mom, I had trouble seeing where it was all going. I remember those long days and longer nights. I remember those homeschooling years when Matthew and I would collide and he would stomp up the stairs and say, "I'm staying up here for the rest of my life!"

I recall one of the many times when he and Ben locked horns and ignored my request to knock it off. I picked up the phone. The boys froze. "You're not calling Dad, are you?" Matt asked.

I certainly was. Captain Fun was commuting for a season, but I knew he would back me up. He has always been my secret weapon. We lived in Vermont at the time, and the Captain sent one son out front to shovel snow and one son out back.

But time changes everything. Matt, a senior (Firstie), and Ben, a freshman (Plebe), were just two floors apart in the barracks Matt's last year. They saw each other fairly often and were intentional about eating together whenever they could. It took some time, but brotherly love, at last, did prevail.

Motherhood is like that. There are days you muddle through it, sometimes with your head in the clouds, other times buried deep in the sand. You mold them, scold them, and ask them how many times you have told them. Then one day the BFE (Big Fat Envelope) comes in the mail, and the light bulb comes on: Of course; he was born to be an army officer.

I remember signing up Mary and Emma for the summer track session to put them *in* something. Only seventeen months apart, they had barely started school, and they both took to it right away. Mary excelled at sprinting and Emma as a distance runner. In Emma's fifth grade year, she was among the first to finish in a 5K. In middle school, Mary was introduced to hurdles and in high school she set records. After over a decade of cross country and track, both girls ran for the Coast Guard Academy. I have loved watching them run; all those hours they put in make so much sense to me now.

Hindsight is 20/20. It is the little things that serve as the foundation for the big things; the ordinary days that bring extraordinary moments. The practices, the meets, overcoming injuries, working through the papers, passing the exams. As parents, it is our job to help them see it through. Not always easy (ask their dad), but always worth it.

The moment when all the work, all the struggle, all those ordinary days combine to form a big picture is upon you before you realize it. That's when, at last, it all makes sense. Though there are days, weeks, and years that parenting seems too monotonous, when it is time for them to leave you, you get it. And they get it.

Then, together, you can bask in the reward, the richness, the wonder of it all.

WHAT A PRIVILEGE ✴

*Delight yourself also in the Lord and He shall give you
the desires of your heart. Commit your way to the Lord,
trust also in Him and He shall bring it to pass.*

PSALM 37:4-5

What a difference twenty years makes.

It had been twenty years since we'd begun attending Bellevue Baptist Church in Memphis. The Captain had scouted out a Sunday school class (there were dozens from which to choose) and it didn't take us long to plug in, making fast friends with other couples who were also trying to decipher how to raise kids. After Sunday school, we sat under the teachings of Dr. Adrian Rogers—truly one of the greatest preachers ever. What a privilege.

By the time number five was on the way, I realized I was in way over my head. I became a regular at the Thursday morning MOMS Bible study with Jean Stockdale. Week after week, I (along with 200 other young moms) sat in that little chapel where she taught Bible passages coupled with parenting principles. Her powerful prayers, hilarious stories, and deep teaching resonated with me.

All those years ago, I didn't know what I didn't know. Still, I began to feel something stir inside of me. Motherhood was my life, and gradually I realized that I wanted to do for other moms what Jean had done for me. And God has allowed me to do just that.

One spring Jean went to Italy (Italy!), to speak to a group of military wives, part of a group called PWOC (Protestant Women of the Chapel). I followed the whole trip on Facebook, thinking (not praying, mind you, just thinking), "Wow, to speak in *Italy.*"

One evening the following fall when I got home, there was a message from my friend Lynn. We had become friends during our Vermont years and our kids went to high school together. "Margie, my daughter's husband is stationed in Italy and heard Jean speak last year. She didn't realize you two knew each other." Pause. I held my breath. "She wondered if you could check your calendar for February and see if you could come speak at next year's retreat."

I exhaled and squealed with enough excitement that my family came running. Whatever was on my calendar was definitely canceled.

The women of the Naples PWOC welcomed me with open arms (and open hearts). I taught four times, from four different passages, and then the Captain and I did a Q&A session. After the retreat was over, we went to Rome to celebrate our upcoming 30th anniversary. I am still pinching myself.

These wonderful women and I laughed together. We cried, we prayed, we embraced. We talked about motherhood and marriage, friendship and faith.

When I think of that little dream that simmered in my heart for all those years, when I think of sitting under Jean for eight years as she not only taught me truths I didn't even know I needed but also modeled how to teach them to others, when I think of how I couldn't have known back then the doors that God would open, when I think that I have been to Italy (*Italy!*) to speak, I am in awe. I am grateful. I am amazed.

What a privilege.

NIGHT AT THE MUSEUM

But as it is written, 'Eye has not seen, nor ear heard, nor have entered into the heart of man the things that God has prepared for those who love Him.' But God has revealed them to us through His Spirit. For the Spirit searches all things, yes, the deep things of God.

I CORINTHIANS 2:9-10

My friend Missy called and asked if we would like to come to dinner. I told her I would check with the Captain and get back with her. Then I started thinking.

"Did you mean just Robert and me, or did you mean all of us?" I texted just to clarify—wouldn't want to surprise them with eight additional guests.

"ALL," came the reply. (Now that didn't happen very often.)

Some of the kids were busy, but that weekend most of the Sims family loaded up and drove out to the country for dinner with our friends.

The house was right out of *Southern Living*, complete with rockers on the massive front porch, lights in the trees, and a tire swing that hung directly in front of a large pond.

It only got better from there. Every corner of the house was decorated in the fall theme, the furnishings were beautiful, and pumpkin scent wafted throughout the house. ("I sprayed it all over just before you came," she said, laughing.)

Our friends had two kids and two foster kids. The little boy had been there for almost a year. We taught him in Sunday school until he promoted out, so we already knew he had made progress. But the night before we came to dinner, they took in another foster child. "We were apprehensive, she was skeptical," they told us, "but we soon fell in love."

I'll call her Jenny. To meet her was to like her, and despite her abusive past, her face radiated a purity and innocence that was refreshing.

As our hungry crowd devoured cheesy meatball subs and watermelon, Mark told us what led them to be foster parents. "I like my peace and quiet, for everything to be in order, like a museum, really," he said, "but we read this book called *Radical* by David Platt, and something stirred in both of us."

"It isn't always easy," Missy chimed in, "but the kids are on board. They wanted to adopt, in fact, even before we started foster parenting. Here we are with two foster kids, and who knows what is in the future. But we are willing to do whatever God leads us to do."

It's true. You never know what will happen when you become willing to do whatever God leads you to do. It is why we had ten kids. It is why Mark and Missy opened their home to children who, in Jenny's own words, "just want to be loved by a family."

After dinner I turned Hope over to her brother Cory so the adults could sit on that lovely porch and get better acquainted. We listened to the crickets, shared stories of how we met, and laughed a lot. Then we called all the kids together and prayed and hugged and said goodbye.

The next day at church during welcome time, Jenny came over to deliver a hug to Mary and Emma. The whole family sat in front of us in church, and I could hardly look at them without tearing up.

Visiting with friends was like a night at the museum. Not the kind of museum Mark and Missy had in mind when they began this journey of surrender, but more like a children's museum—you might get a little messy, but you sure learn a lot, and it's way more fun.

"It's chaos sometimes," our friends said, "but there is nowhere else we would rather be."

THE SECRET SAUCE ✦

And one of them, when he saw that he was healed,
returned, and with a loud voice glorified God, and fell down
on his face at His feet, giving Him thanks. And he was a
Samaritan. So Jesus answered and said, 'Were there not ten
cleansed? But where are the nine? Were there not any found
who returned to give glory to God except this foreigner?'

LUKE 17:15-18

When Mary and Emma began the trip home from their mission trip to Peru, the plan was to return on Saturday. However, when the flight was canceled twice, it was yet another reminder that the whole experience had been a crash course in gratitude.

The girls boarded the plane in Lima on time for a midnight departure, but the pilot soon announced a delay. "About four hours later, we deboarded the plane, having had only a little water and even less sleep, plus a whole lot of stress," their leader wrote in an update to the folks back home.

I was relieved when Mary messaged me. "You must be exhausted," I replied when she told me her version of the story.

"I am tired, but learning to give thanks anyway." If that wasn't enough, she went on, reflecting on her trip. "At least my life doesn't consist of working all day in a field by the time I turn seven."

"Hola, Mom!" Emma inserted her thoughts. "The weirdest things I have eaten are cow heart, guinea pig, and cactus fruit," she wrote, as if she were stating that grass is green and the sky is blue.

Messaging with my daughters took me back to my own mission trip to Belize in 1983. I was seventeen and had never even been on a plane before. Primitive toilets, bathing in the river, fire ants, food smothered in pungent cheese, soldiers everywhere... The list is endless. I have never forgotten the impact that such exposure to poverty and hardship had on me, and I have never been so grateful as I was for the one warm shower I had during the two weeks I was there.

Gratitude: perhaps some kids keep it easier than others, but all kids need it. Just how do you instill, enforce, and encourage it? There are lots of ways in this culture—loads of privileges to remove should you see an ungrateful mindset creeping in. Whether it is to the inner city or halfway around the world, letting kids see, touch, serve, and work among those who have less… Well, let's just say when they are thankful for the cow heart on their plates or that they don't have to work in a field all day, gratitude is present.

I am so proud of those girls. Proud of their growth, flexibility and, yes, their attitude of gratitude. They possessed it when they went; they returned with even more. After their return, I saw it spilling out onto the whole family. Even their younger sister declared that while counseling and medication have their place, perhaps a good dose of exposure to those less fortunate would be the prescription for some of her middle school cohorts.

Gratitude is the secret ingredient, the watershed, the approach to life that changes everything. Sometimes kids only need a little encouragement to feel it, sometimes it must be forced upon them.

After all, if Jesus asked the one returning leper where the other nine went, we better be questioning the level of our own kids' gratitude, too.

SUPERMAN

...the glory of children is their father.

PROVERBS 17:6b

Every year as Father's Day approaches, I brainstorm for something that will do Captain Fun justice. What in the world can be done for the father of ten? How can we say we love you, we need you, we thank you, and we couldn't do life without you?

The year yet another Superman movie released, Bethany suggested it was only natural to give Father's Day a Superman theme. (Thank you, Bethany!) After all, what better word to describe their dad?

On Father's Day, I like to have presents waiting for the Captain after lunch, and lunch is always the biggest, thickest steak I can find— but only for him; the rest of us eat a cheaper cut. Superman needs his sustenance.

Some of the presents were symbolic of why he was still our Superman. Some were just because they fit the job description.

First on the list, *True Grit*, starring none other than the Duke himself. (Not all men have it. You've got it, Captain.) I also found a copy of one of his favorite movies—*Chariots of Fire*. It is about conviction and the pace required to run the race. By this point we had been raising kids for nearly three decades—still changing diapers while many of our friends had empty nests. I owe him a huge *thank you* for running this marathon beside me.

Next, an authentic Yankee Clipper sled: $9 at Goodwill. For years the Captain had been trying to describe to our kids the sled of our generation: wooden with a little boomerang shaped steering contraption at the front, and up on steel runners. (You don't want to find yourself in its path.) It was my favorite find in a very long time. I was going to wait until Christmas, but what if it snowed in November? He was truly surprised, something not easily done.

Two books: *Dutch*, about Ronald Reagan, and *The Boys of '98*, about Theodore Roosevelt's Rough Riders. These are two of our favorite presidents. The Captain and I love presidential history—we visited Monticello for a recent anniversary, in fact.

Basketball goal. We had been without one since we left New York. The Captain missed shooting hoops with the kids.

Baseball glove from Cory, #7, who made the little league All-Star team. "Dad mentioned he is going to get himself a new glove whenever we practice," Cory told me. I am impressed that not only was he paying attention, but he also used his own money.

Coffee. For the Keurig machine at work, from Ben, #4. Even Superman needs a recharge in the afternoon.

Family picture, framed and mounted. I have been known to buy and hang frames with the models still in them. They look like nice folks, after all. But now the frame I bought proudly displayed us and our ten kids (daughter-in-law Becky had to work that day). He took it to the office to keep him company.

Superhero Mask. Made by Silas, #9, his last week of kindergarten. "You are my hero," he wrote on the back. Fit perfectly with the theme, thank you.

A kayak, from daughter Bethany, #2. Captain Fun put her through college, and she says thank you every chance she gets. Tiger, #1, called right before she gave it to her dad, so he got to watch on Facetime. "I'm the favorite," she said to him through a smile. The debate continues.

A bird feeder and birdseed, bases and a kickball from Emma, #6, and from Mary, #5, a beach towel and goggles. Emma and her dad find a lot of pleasure in bird watching together. As far as the ball and bases, towel and goggles, we don't call him Captain Fun for nothing.

Matthew, #3, gave him a workout shirt and a book, *The Cost of Discipleship* by Dietrich Bonhoeffer so the Captain could follow his physical workout with a spiritual workout.

Dorothy, #8, bought him his favorite Almond Joy/Mounds candy but left it in her room where Hope, #10, was sleeping. That one had to wait.

We topped it all off with an Almond Joy cake (my Aunt Marilyn's recipe) and some movie tickets to see the latest Superman movie, and there you had it: Father's Day for our Superman.

We all knew what he would say when we called him Superman and showered him with gifts: "God is the real Superman; it is only through Christ that I am who I am."

That is why we love him so.

BABY

For everyone who partakes only of milk is unskilled in the word of righteousness, for he is a babe. But solid food belongs to those who are of full age, that is, who by reason of use have their senses to exercise to discern both good and evil.

HEBREWS 5: 13-14

Because I am the youngest of eight, my parents and siblings have referred to me as the baby ever since I can remember.

I have ten kids. I have been pregnant for approximately seven years of my life, spent over a hundred hours in labor, and have changed thousands of diapers. But no matter what I do, to my siblings I will always be the baby. I have never understood it. Until Hope came along.

It could be because I had her when I was closer to 50 than 40. Or maybe it was because the whole family doted on her. (She's everybody's baby, I often said.) Or it might even be because I knew she was probably my last one. But there was something about that baby that made me want to keep her a baby.

At her fifteen-month check-up, I sheepishly explained to the pediatrician why she was not yet walking. She had so many people who carried her around, we didn't put her down long enough for her to learn how to walk. My friend who was a physical therapist confirmed it during an impromptu evaluation. Hope only needed to get her balance, she said.

Then I felt compelled to defend why she was still drinking a bottle. I had two trips planned, you see, and the bottle sure kept her quiet. (People on airplanes like quiet babies.) As soon as those trips were behind me, I would get her off that bottle.

It was true. I took her to Vermont when I spoke at a women's breakfast. Then two weeks later we went to Memphis to see my family. That's when it hit me: Hope is not a baby.

The first day we were in Memphis, she was content to sit in my lap and drink her bottle. (That's the way I like it.) But she soon had to be part of the action. By the next day her second cousin Henry, six months older, showed her how to climb and push little trucks across the window sill.

Once we got back home, her siblings agreed she was older, more mature, less like a baby. Sigh. I supposed it was time.

I stretched Hope's infancy out as far as it would go, but then realized I must allow her, assist her, and equip her to move on.

The Christian life is like that. Content to sit and watch, we resist growth, change, or anything that stretches our faith. But, unlike the way I babied Hope, the Heavenly Father won't let us remain as infants. He will do what He must to help us grow, move on and find our balance.

When He does, just like Hope, maturity is certain.

✦ THIS IS A TEST

Count it all joy when you fall into various trials,
knowing that the testing of your faith produces
patience. But let patience have its perfect work, that
you may be perfect and complete, lacking nothing.

JAMES 1:2-4

If we make it to March 1st without any significant illnesses, I always breathe a sigh of relief.

I recall one year, however, on March 2nd, Hope came down with a stomach virus. We had company coming—friends from Vermont. Our friend Karl Swanke played for Green Bay in the '80's, (#67—look him up) and his visit was perfectly timed with our church's March Madness sports theme. He planned to say a few words at church while he and his wife, Maggie (one of my favorite people), were with us for the weekend, college shopping with their daughter. I texted them with the news of Hope's illness. They came anyway and, as usual, were a breath of fresh air.

The Swankes left right after church, and by sundown the other seven kids and Captain Fun had fallen ill. You haven't lived until you have seven kids throwing up at the same time. Though, truth be told, the older five and the Captain were on their own, poor things, as I had to take care of Dorothy and Silas. All I could do was listen to hurried footsteps all night while I tended to the younger ones. Thankfully, our friends escaped it.

Ten days later, Dorothy woke up with a headache and high fever. For three days, she lay on the couch, missing the whole week of school.

Tiger and Matt, my two oldest sons, had the same spring break and planned to spend it at our house. I was elated to have all ten kids under the same roof. Within 48 hours of arriving, the stomach bug bit them. I brought them Sprite and crackers. It was just like old times, we joked. Somehow both agreed it was still a great visit home—one of the best, even, minus that twenty-four hours.

Within a day of their departure, Hope woke up from her nap feverish, inconsolable, and lethargic. I rushed her to the doctor. Influenza B, he confirmed, and wrote a prescription for Tamiflu at $100 a pop. For almost a week she lay on my chest, not smiling, not playing, not eating. I had never had an infant with the flu before. I acted as if she was my first child, calling the nurse three times in the same day. I worried. I prayed. While Dorothy could tell me how she was feeling, all Hope could do was rest her head on my shoulder and cry. I thought of parents who have seriously ill children and wondered how they endured.

"I hope you don't get it," the doctor had said to me.

"Oh, I don't worry too much about getting it," I said, ignoring the tickle in my throat. By day three, the flu hit me full force. "I can see why you didn't get off the couch for three days," I told Dorothy. On the day Hope and I were at our worst, a construction crew arrived in front of my house complete with jack hammers, waking her up from her much-needed nap and allowing no relief for my pounding head.

By the time Hope recovered, Cory was down, calling for another $100 prescription and missed week of school. He returned to class after three days, and Mom Dot spent three days in bed. Captain Fun checked on her, I checked on her, the kids checked on her. Soup, cold medicine, water and more water. At last, she poked her head out of her bedroom door, "Just to let you know I am still alive."

Why the stomach bug and the flu in the same month? Why when we had so much company planned? (I even had a big birthday bash planned for sweet cousin Ellen that I had to cancel—twice.)

"Count it all joy when you fall into trials," the book of James says. Well, I am not quite celebrating trials yet, but I do know you just have to roll with them, let them stretch you, grow you, remind you that being there for each other is what family is for. It's no fun, as that particular year the month of March seemed three months long. But someone said we can let things make us bitter or better, and at least if we let it grow us, the experience is not wasted.

Once in a while when I was a kid, a strange man's voice would interrupt the *Brady Bunch*. "This is a test. This is only a test," he said before an annoying buzz would take over the TV for sixty seconds.

I still hear that voice during times of trial: this is only a test.

GAIT CHANGES ✦

Jesus Christ is the same yesterday, today and forever.
HEBREWS 13:8

After having ten kids in the span of twenty-five years, I frequently feel stuck in a time warp much like Bill Murray in *Groundhog Day*. As soon as one child gained a little independence, another arrived. But, at this end of motherhood, I have had such a sense of time and the inevitable changes it brings. When nearly half the kids had left the nest, three more were perched on the branch, preparing to fly. Some still a few years away, but I knew it would seem like no time at all.

Looking out the window on the way to church one Sunday morning, I caught a glimpse of an elderly gentleman ambling toward a cemetery. He was dressed in his Sunday best.

Hands in his pockets, his gait was slow, a mere shuffle. Even though I only saw him from a distance, I was struck by his seeming sadness.

Maybe it was because another anniversary of my mother's death was approaching. Anyone who has lost their mom is familiar with the emotion it evokes. Even running across one of her favorite brands while shopping the previous week had made me teary. Hard for me to believe that my four youngest would have no memory of my mother. It seemed impossible that she had been gone for over a decade.

Or perhaps it was that Hope was now a toddler with four teeth popping through and already calling some of her siblings by name. Slow down, I urged her—and the rest of the family agreed. Well, except Silas, maybe.

"These are the best years of your life, with all the kids around your feet," my dad once told me. Many years have passed since he offered that advice, and I still had plenty of kids underfoot. But my perspective had changed. I'd shifted from thinking that nothing ever changes to knowing everything does.

I guess time has taught me that life consists of a series of changes. Some come suddenly, and some so gradually that I don't notice until they are upon me, staring me in the face. I am finally starting to get it, and it has caused me to brake where I used to accelerate, to amble instead of rush. Much like the dear old man in the cemetery, my gait has changed from mad dash to a slow and steady saunter. If I had stopped to ask his viewpoint, I am certain he would have given me a charge to live more deliberately, more intentionally along the way.

I sure am trying.

LET US PRAY ✴

In this manner, therefore, pray...
MATTHEW 6:9a

I remember Mary coming home in tears over a school shooting, like so many other students across the country have at different times, when she was in eighth grade. I will not begin to approach the reasons for random shootings. There is no explaining the senseless killing of innocent people.

But, like I told Mary, the one thing we can do daily and diligently is pray. The victims' families have a long road ahead of them. In a week or two the media moves on and these families are left alone with their losses.

Here is how I pray over senseless acts of violence. Feel free to join me.

● Pray for the young survivors who witnessed the death of their friends and teachers. They have their whole lives ahead of them— they must heal. Pray that their parents and extended family will know how to help them.

● Pray for the churches of the community. Pray for pastors, Sunday school teachers and children's ministry directors, that they would be able to be strong. There will not be a Sunday that passes that they will not be grieved over the empty seats in their classrooms.

● Pray for the area counselors over the next year. Pray that they would have keen insight and wisdom and would not say anything harmful, but only words that help.

- Pray for the many funerals that have to take place in the commu nity. Pray for those who speak and sing. Pray for the funeral directors and for the people who attend. Pray, too, that somehow God's presence and peace would prevail.
- Pray that the survivors would be spared the thoughtless words from well-meaning (but thought-less) people. Job's friends spent forty chapters trying to explain to him why he lost his children, only to have God Himself rebuke them. "My wrath is aroused against you and your two friends, for you have not spoken of Me what is right, as My servant Job has. (Job 42:7b)"
- Pray for the school adminis-trators to have unity and wisdom about when and where and how to start school again. Pray for the interim principal that he/she would be able to lead the faculty, staff, parents and students with strength, wisdom and composure.
- Pray for our nation's leaders, that they would unite in wisdom and purpose to bring answers for all and not fuel their own agendas.
- Pray for our nation's families. Everything that affects our culture, I believe, begins and ends with the family.
- Pray for the families of the victims, of course, to find com-fort. Pray for the marriages to withstand the pressure of such a terrible tragedy. Statistics are against them.
- Pray as holidays and anniversa-ries approach. The first holidays, anniversaries, and birthdays will be agony for them, but every year will be difficult.

Jesus said in Matthew 18:20, "For where two or three are gathered to-gether in My name, I am there in the midst of them." Let us remember to gather in our hour of darkness and pray to the Light.

Section Three:
FAMILY

"And the fruit of the Spirit is love, joy, peace, longsuffering, kindness, goodness, faithfulness, gentleness and self-control," Galatians 5:22 reminds us. The "Nine Divine" are accessible to everyone. In all my years of being a wife and a mom, I have concluded that healthy family relationships are impossible without them.

FIRE? WHAT FIRE?

*But the fruit of the Spirit is love, joy, peace, longsuffering,
kindness, goodness, faithfulness, gentleness, self-control.
Against such there is no law.*

GALATIANS 5:22-23

I awakened well before dawn one morning when we still lived in that wonderful old house in New York.

Sniff, sniff. *Is that smoke?* I thought. No, just dust on the heater after it's been off all summer. The nights had begun to get nippy, as my dad used to say, and the heat had been due to come on.

I laid there for a while, when suddenly Captain Fun jumped out of bed. "Do you smell smoke?" he asked, controlled urgency in his voice.

Having been awake for some time, I was getting sleepy. "No." I rolled over to finally doze off. "It is just the heater coming on after being off all summer. It's the dust burning off."

He left the room to return with a flashlight. "Look!" he said, aiming the beam over my head. "That is smoke."

"Where? I don't see any smoke." I was so sleepy, after all.

"Could you get up and help me look around?"

He asked so politely, it was the least I could do.

He went toward the boys' bedroom; I headed into the den. As I looked up at the light fixture, there was no mistaking it. A little bit of smoke was slowly seeping into the room from the attic. I woke up.

"Honey!" I ran to the bedroom. "Come take a look at this!"

"Get the kids up!" he said, as he headed to the attic to take a look. I made the rounds. I was on it. I was alert. I was in.

He came down from the attic to find us headed for the door. "Well, I found the fire and was able to put it out." He explained that an old electrical box had apparently shorted and ignited itself. "You guys go back to bed and I will stay up just in case," adding that he would call someone first thing in the morning.

I had barely closed my eyes, it seemed, when he woke me up. "You know, I am afraid of that old box re-igniting, so I am going up to check. You might want to get up in case we have to clear out suddenly."

Against my will, I got up, but that word "might" got stuck in my head and I convinced myself I had time to jump in the shower. Just as I got out of the shower, Captain Fun told me that the fire had reignited in the attic and he had called 911. I needed to hurry.

Surely I had time to dry my hair, I thought. It wouldn't take long.

When Captain Fun came back a third time and found me drying my hair, let's just say he stopped being Captain Fun for a moment. "Turn that off and get in the car. Now."

Was it necessary to be so harsh? Surely not. I had gone through labor nine times without so much as raising my voice. Surely this harshness was uncalled for.

I obediently got into the car. He had already loaded up the kids and Mom Dot. As I backed out of the garage, I could hardly believe my eyes. Smoke hovered above the roof of our house from one end to the other. "Honey, look at the smoke!" I said, so distracted, in fact, that I backed into his Mustang.

"I know," he said. "That's what I have been trying to tell you. The. House. Is. On. Fire."

I drove down the hill with the kids and Mom Dot and, as the Captain had suggested, we headed to McDonald's for breakfast. We passed the fire truck on our way. The firemen were quick and careful, keeping damage contained to one room. Thank the Lord that because Captain Fun acted so quickly, no one was injured.

Why did it take me so long to realize the house was on fire? Again, when my husband said I might want to get up, I got stuck on that word "might." Even though I had seen the smoke and heard the urgency in his voice, I was hoping maybe it wasn't as serious as all that.

Maybe it is too easy to take the same approach with our families. We see the smoke: negligence, apathy, all the other red flags that pop up when a relationship is deteriorating. We hear the urgency in our children's or spouse's voice when they hint something isn't right. But we just won't accept that, yes, the house is on fire.

I hope I always remember what I learned that day: where there's smoke, there's fire. Though that fire was traumatic, it could have been much worse had Captain Fun not been so quick to respond when he saw the smoke. May I handle my family with the same urgency.

After all, far more than a house, a family is worth it.

✳A COMMON GOAL

Like an apple tree among the trees of the woods, so is my beloved
among the sons. I sat down in his shade with great delight, and his
fruit was sweet to my taste.

SONG OF SOLOMON 2:3

"You have to come meet this girl at my church," my husband's best friend told him one day many years ago. "She is the female version of you."

According to Robert, he came and we were introduced, though I don't recall that first conversation. The second conversation, however, got my attention.

I rode my ten speed to the store. As I was leaving, he was on the payphone—if you can remember those. "Hey," he called to me, "don't we go to church together?"

He had caught my eye by then, and I was glad to confirm that we did, indeed, attend the same church. He said he had been going to Union University, but had just transferred to Memphis because his dad's cancer had returned. When he wasn't running the family trucking business, he was part of a prison ministry. I was impressed—which he later confessed to be his goal. As I pedaled away, I said a little prayer about that guy on the payphone.

Soon after, his dad's illness took a turn for the worse. While other friends from church visited the hospital to show their support, I kept my distance, afraid of sending the wrong message since I barely knew him. His dad was in ICU for over a month before he passed away. I regret that I never met him.

After his father's death, Robert stepped up to the plate— going to school full time, hauling cotton samples across the country to keep the Sims Sample Service family business going, and trying to be there for his mom through her grief—all at nineteen years old.

For the next six months, I watched. I waited. Occasionally I caught a glimpse of him at church. He was always late, coming in off the road from delivering samples to customers. He later told me he sometimes ate coffee grounds right out of the can to stay awake. Though he hardly made it to class that year, he still kept a 3.8 GPA.

One Spring morning as I was leaving class, I remembered him mentioning he met a mutual friend of ours at the library every day to give her a ride home. Clearly the opportunity to speed things up had presented itself. I moseyed on over to the library.

I soon heard a familiar voice. "Hey, Margie! What are you doing here? Have you seen Robert?"

"Robert? No, is he, *ahem*, supposed to be here?" I said, just as he walked up. Goal in sight.

"Hey, we were about to go to lunch," he said, with that irresistible smile. "Want to come along?"

"As a matter of fact, I do." I later confessed that was my goal.

Within a few weeks, he asked me to dinner. The friendship grew, and six months later we were engaged—which was my ultimate goal.

"You and Dad make it look so easy," oldest daughter Bethany said once.

"I wouldn't call it easy," I told her, "but when you are committed and you love each other, you keep a common goal in mind."

Like everyone else, our life together has been a series of changes. We have endured the loss of both my parents, many miscarriages, many moves. Through it all, though, we repeatedly return to the common goal, the big picture.

I love you, Captain. I would do it all over again with you. And that will never change.

✦ WHAT A MOTHER WANTS

A word fitly spoken is like apples of gold in settings of silver.
PROVERBS 25:11

"What do you want for Mother's Day?" Emma asked one year as that glorious day approached.

"Dark chocolate covered almonds," I said. "Dove or above."

When I used to ask my mother this question, she would always give the same answer: "I already have everything I want."

Don't you know that you are going to miss the chance for all the loot? I would think. She had eight kids. That's eight presents. Even I could do that math.

I either got her a present—an eggbeater or a half dead flower—or drew her a picture. She always raved about it.

Mother's Day has always been a big deal around here thanks to Captain Fun. I woke up that year to find a new laptop from the Captain himself. He has always been my biggest fan.

I knew from past Mother's Days that being the mom of so many meant lots more loot coming— three pounds of chocolate and three pounds of coffee—and I still had three more kids to hear from.

"Matt said to get on the Bed, Bath & Beyond website and order yourself some thousand thread-count sheets," Captain Fun told me after breakfast (French toast and blackberries with squirty whipped cream, I'll have you know).

"Wow, really?" The thought of thousand count sheets almost made me choke on my blackberries. Matt had been away at Vermont National Guard boot camp and medic training for six months, but somehow he remembered I said I would buy some one day.

Two calls after church from Tiger and Bethany announced more surprises arriving the following day. Nine kids, nine gifts. And a new laptop. That really was a lot of loot.

Do I enjoy the presents? Yes, I do. When my kids ask me what I want, I tell them—chocolate, coffee, pajamas, expensive shampoo. All those little pampering gifts that most moms enjoy.

But it isn't all the stuff that a mother really wants, though that's a definite perk. It's the affirmation behind the stuff: thank you, you're appreciated, we notice what you do.

"I don't know what I would do without you," read Emma's card. I almost teared up a little at her words. *That's* what a mother really wants.

SISTERS

Now it happened as they went that He entered a certain village; and a certain woman named Martha welcomed Him into her house. And she had a sister called Mary, who also sat at Jesus' feet and heard His word.

LUKE 10:38-39

"Don't worry, Bethany," I told my oldest daughter after the birth of her third brother. "No matter how many times I have to try, I am going to make sure you have a sister." That was three sisters ago.

Sisters really are that important in my book. One special weekend I was once again reminded why. My sister right above me had turned fifty, so the six of us girls gathered near Atlanta to celebrate with her. We drank pots of coffee to coincide with our hours of conversation. We painted nails, shopped, went to lunch, and caught each other up on our kids.

One evening we were laughing about our upbringing. "Did you *ever* get a spanking, Margie?" one of them asked. I assured them I did—a total of three that I can remember, but I'm not sure if they believed me.

"I can remember Daddy telling me I didn't need college, but I better learn to type," my oldest sister laughed, adding that they were always afraid to ask him for a quarter for gas.

I had a gas credit card, I teased. Well, not really, but I never remember feeling afraid to ask my dad for money. It is no secret, after all, that I had a different upbringing than they did. Not that my parents were rich, just established. By the time number eight came along, they were more relaxed.

"Now that I see all of our girls growing up together, I am starting to get that sister thing," Captain Fun said to me as I was preparing for my trip. It's true, sisters have a thing. We fight over the lunch check, laugh with each other, bicker with each other, but always, always forgive each other. Mama would have wanted it that way, we agree.

At Binghamton airport, my daughters clamored out of the car to greet me upon my return home. After a light tackle, they chatted about their day at the mall, lunch at Subway and how they got flip flops BOGO. Ordinary stuff, yes, but sisters care about that sort of thing as much as they care about life's more serious issues.

"I don't know what I would do without five sisters to share in Mom's care," I remember one of my sisters saying during my mother's bout with cancer.

She needed round the clock care for the last eight months of her life, and I learned the same lesson then that I was reminded of last weekend. Much like Martha and Mary, sisters may not always agree with each other, but whether it's sharing a burden or sharing dessert, sisters are there, ready to help, laugh, cry or celebrate.

That's what sisters do. That's what sisters are for.

BIG ENOUGH

He will bless those who fear the Lord, both small and great. May
the Lord give you increase more and more, you and your children.
May you be blessed by the Lord, who made heaven and earth.

PSALM 115: 13-15

A man approached me one day as I was climbing into my van in New York City. "Is this the airport shuttle?"

"No," I said, before he could toss in his bag. "Just my family car." When you have as many kids as I do, you are used to everything being big, both in number and in size. Two hotel rooms, three car seats, four pizzas.

Back when I had only nine kids, I was attending the American Society of Journalists and Authors conference. Jane—my friend, writing coach, cheerleader, and *Memphis Parent* editor—suggested we go when I told her I lived so close to the city.

Going to New York City for a writer's conference made me feel big time. Until I got there. The place was buzzing with energy and swarming with writers. Suddenly, being in New York City made me feel small.

"What do you do for a living?" I asked one particularly chatty woman.

She looked at me quizzically. "I write."

Oh. You mean you can *do* that?

The keynote was a pioneer mom blogger and five time book author, a Huggies, Hershey, Pull-Ups spokesperson, as well as a guest on *The Today Show*, *The Early Show*, and practically every show in between.

I left the conference feeling quite small and unaccomplished. Until I got into my van to go home. There

I was, The Big, Bad Mama, cutting my twelve-passenger straight through the New York City traffic. No matter that it was Sunday morning and traffic was minimal. It still counted.

My van is one representation of, for lack of a better word, the bigness of my family. No, I am not a big time writer, but the mom of a big time family who has a little time to write.

That is big enough for me.

 HOMECOMINGS

Where no oxen are, the trough is clean, but much
increase comes by the strength of the ox.

PROVERBS 14:4

A return from a trip reminded me how much I love homecomings.

Emma and Mary, ages twelve and thirteen, stalked my car to see who could touch me first when I opened the door.

"I missed your coffee," said Mom Dot, delivering a hug.

"Oh, Mommy, I am so glad you're home," said Emma. That made me feel good. "We have been out of milk for two days, and I had frozen casserole for lunch and dinner."

Thank you, I think.

Captain Fun embraced me, kissed me, said I was a rock star.

"Did you notice I took out the trash?" asked Ben, fifteen at the time.

Dorothy, my then-six-year-old, begged for a spot on my lap during family devotions, after which I cleaned the kitchen, did some laundry, swept the floor, cleaned out the fridge, and took some steaks out to thaw for a real dinner.

In my younger years, I would have gone on a rant (to which no one would have listened) about all the work I do and why it should still get done even when I am not here to do it. But the older I get, the less I mind being needed for the many roles I play.

"Where no oxen are, the crib is clean," Proverbs 14:4 says, "but much increase comes by the strength of the ox." That verse always makes me chuckle when I think of my kids. Where no kids are, the house is clean.

Family life might be messy (when I'm away, it's really messy), but I'll take it. I returned refreshed, ready for the hugs, the work, and everything else that awaited me.

It's a good thing—those homecomings can be a lot of work.

✴ A GOOD SIGN

Show me a sign for good, that those who hate me may see it and be ashamed. Because You, Lord, have helped me and comforted me.

PSALM 86:17

I have never been very good at hiding things. At Christmas, for instance, I toss all the presents in a corner of my bedroom and throw a blanket over the pile. Not too obvious, right?

So when I shoved my prenatal vitamins into the closet, still wrapped in the Rite-Aid bag, I thought the kids wouldn't notice. I forgot that Mary never misses a beat.

"Mom! Mom!" she hollered, dragging me back to the hall closet. "I found these vitamins next to the children's vitamins (oops) and they say 'For pregnant and lactating women,' and I had to go ask Grandmama, 'What does *lactating* mean?' and then she told me I had to come find you and…Mom, are you *pregnant?*"

I nodded, unable to speak for laughing. She threw her arms around me for a long hug. Emma darted out of the bathroom and joined us. "I was listening." The gig was up. I couldn't hide it.

Not that I wanted to hide it. A baby is a blessing. A gift. A sign for good. But I had miscarried the last two and wanted to go to the doctor before I told the kids. At last, I saw the little six-week-old jelly bean with (sigh of relief) a heartbeat. Then like a good mommy I went and bought my prenatal vitamins loaded with folic acid.

"Maybe I'll have a flower girl!" said Bethany, who was certain that seven-year-old Dorothy would be too old by the time she got married.

"Awesome," said Matthew, who

was soon bound for the West Point Prep school.

"Y'all are crazy," said Tiger, my oldest, who had remained constant in this opinion the last three babies. But I am certain he loves being the oldest of ten. My goal had been to not be pregnant at his wedding the previous summer, I reminded him. Mission accomplished. Now if I could be done before he started a family of his own. He assured me that mission is also easily accomplished, as no such plans were in the works.

Dorothy, who said she was praying for a baby sister, was beaming. Cory beamed, too, in his own quiet way. Ben and Mom Dot both agreed that another baby is a blessing. In fact, the vote was unanimous in our family.

Well, except for Silas, who did not acknowledge it when we told him the news. Perhaps he was busy calculating how much his life was about to change.

Our family had been through a rough patch over the previous year. I know many wouldn't agree, but we considered a baby a good sign.

"Let's name her Hope if it's a girl," my husband said to me the day we found out. I loved the idea.

While, yes, there was plenty I could worry about, news of a baby had brought new energy, excitement, and yes, hope, to the Sims family.

In my estimation, that's a good sign.

 BIRTHDAYS

Pleasant words are like a honeycomb,
sweetness to the soul and health to the bones.
PROVERBS 16:24

Celebrating my birthday always gets me to thinking about how birthdays change as we get older.

When I was younger, I was focused on the gifts—a grooming set, a new pair of boots, a cowboy hat—anything that would better equip me to care for or enjoy my horse. I shared my mom's birthday as well as my grandfather's, but as far as I can remember, the focus was usually on me, the baby. I am sure my sisters would agree.

Now that I am grown with kids of my own, I enjoy simple luxuries on my birthday: chocolate (Dove or above, thank you), a homemade poster of everyone's hand prints (Emma thought of that herself), dozens of good wishes from Facebook, an uninterrupted nap. I was thrilled with the walk on the beach with Captain Fun the year we were brand new Florida residents. (My daughter-in-law suggested we go and leave all the kids with her and Tiger. I love that girl.)

Then there is my favorite birthday tradition: What I Like About You. It's obvious, I think, that this is where everyone in the family tells the birthday person what they like about them. The year of my 46th birthday, it held special meaning.

"You're patient," said Ben, and I was amazed that one of the kids usually said this. I am always glad to hear it—especially that year. Expecting my tenth child at age 46, I didn't feel patient.

"You give us what we need when

we are young so that by the time we are grown, we are ready to stand on our own," Matt and Tiger both agreed. Phew—this was good to hear, as I had been feeling a little negligent of my older ones.

"You cook me food," said Cory, always the practical one. Considering he has to eat whatever I fix, vegetables and all, I took this as a compliment.

Bethany called from school and said she loved our friendship. Emma thanked me for everything I do; Mary said I was funny; Dorothy said I am pretty—even with my new beach ball shape. Silas said I was… squishy. Eight out of nine wasn't bad, I supposed. I accepted it.

That particular year I turned the tables after the tradition was over. "Now let me tell you what I like about you," I said. "You are my treasures, my greatest gifts. Whenever someone asks me about my kids, you should hear me brag on each one of you."

"I never thought about that," said Ben.

I have always said a woman needs three things to feel appreciated on her birthday: a meal she doesn't have to make, a cake she doesn't have to bake, and a gift to open—no matter how small.

I still hold to that. We women are the ones who usually bend over backwards to make everyone else's birthdays special, and it's nice when it's our turn and someone else does the bending.

But these past few years as I have sat around the table with both my adult and younger kids, I finally get what my mother used to say when I would ask her what she wanted on her birthday:

I have everything I need.

 HELLO, HOPE

Better is a dinner of herbs where love is,
than a fatted calf with hatred.

PROVERBS 15:17

Ten times I have gone into the hospital to deliver a baby, and with each one I have had two events that I anticipate more than anything else.

The first, of course, is the moment the baby arrives and my husband and I simultaneously laugh and cry at the wonder of it all. No matter how many times we go through it, the experience still leaves us in awe.

While I love ordering my food and receiving it on that wonderful tray that hangs right over my bed, and I certainly relish the forty-eight hours where I can hold, feed, and stare at the baby in isolation and silence, another event trumps these: The moment when my other kids come to the hospital to meet their new sibling for the first time. Hope's birth was no exception.

Bethany is always the first one to get her hands on the baby. In her twenty years of meeting new brothers and sisters, she has practically become a professional baby handler.

"You have another baby in your tummy?" asked four-year-old Silas. One of them never fails to ask. He pushed on my stomach to see if it was firm like when Hope was inside. It wasn't. He moved on, spotting all those buttons on my bed.

Seven-year-old Dorothy was all snaggle-toothed smiles. She was surrounded by brothers in her birth order and finally had a baby sister all her own.

Ben and Cory took to Hope immediately and patiently waited for their turn to hold her. I liked seeing this tenderness in my boys.

All four girls eventually gathered around the bassinet and stared at Hope. It was a magical moment and I memorized the wonder on their faces.

"I am Hope in my family," I said, reminding them that when I was born, two of my oldest sisters were 14 and 12, the same age as Mary and Emma at the time of Hope's birth. She couldn't possibly know it yet, but little Hope was in for a lot of love.

Hello, Hope. Welcome to the family.

BROTHERS AND SISTERS

*Behold, how good and how pleasant it is for
brethren to dwell together in unity!*

PSALM 133:1

For as long as I can remember, I have been surrounded by people. With two brothers and five sisters, a crowd was unavoidable. Even after the nest began to empty, my mother was very deliberate about gathering the family: Christmas, Easter, and a weekly Sunday fried chicken dinner if my memory serves me correctly.

It wasn't until I was about fifteen that I realized the toothbrush holder in the bathroom was almost bare. Only my brother's and mine remained, and I didn't like it. Then when I was seventeen, my brother moved out and took his toothbrush with him. It was my parents and me—a strange and lonely feeling.

"I hate being alone," I once overheard a mom say, adding that it must be because she was an only child.

While I cannot say that I dislike being alone (I seek out a little solitude every day, in fact), the older I get, the more I realize what a gift my parents gave my siblings and me simply by having so many of us. My parents have been gone for years now, but my brothers and sisters and I still have each other.

We have always had each other. Through my mom's cancer, my dad's Alzheimer's, and every happy and sad occasion in between.

"Did you name your youngest Hope because you hope it's the last one?" someone once humorously suggested. I laughed. It was funny.

But, no. This one is called Hope because she came along at a trying

144

time in the Sims family. "A bright spot of hope," Captain Fun so articulately said from the moment we found out she was on the way.

Though I know it's not for everyone, I like to think we are giving our kids the same gift my parents gave me: the gift of knowing that long after Captain Fun and I are gone, they will still have each other.

 "A" DAY

> *You, therefore, must endure hardship as a good*
> *soldier of Jesus Christ. No one engaged in warfare*
> *entangles himself with the affairs of this life, that he*
> *may please him who enlisted him to be a soldier.*
>
> 2 TIMOTHY 2:3-4

I am at a loss for words to describe how I felt the weekend Captain Fun and I (with five month old Hope in tow) traveled to the USMA at West Point for Matthew's long anticipated "A" Day. But here's the best list I could come up with.

Moved: When the band played and the companies marched, I thought of my dad and how proud he would be. He was a Navy man, and he loved the military. For someone who never made it to high school, it opened up the world to him. I tried to think of what he would say at seeing his grandson admitted to West Point. I can hear my mother, "That's first class, Marge, that's first class." But my dad was a man of few words, and he probably would have gotten *that look* on his face, and I would know.

Proud: After the ceremony, we had Matthew all to ourselves for the better part of two days. (Well, Hope was in on it, too.) Matt was required to wear his uniform, and everywhere we went—from the funky Fiddlesticks Cafe in tiny Cornwall, New York, to the Metropolitan Museum of Art in New York City—the uniform commanded admiration and attention. I thought about getting a t-shirt with an arrow that said *I'm his mom*, but I restrained myself.

Tickled: Captain Fun and I agreed—it was hilarious that we had a son at West Point while simultaneously parenting an infant. We heard it over and over that weekend. "Is that *your* baby?" Yes, we answered repeatedly, she's number ten, our cadet is number three. There are ten in all. It's hard to explain. Folks told us we were blessed. We agreed on that, too.

Inspired: Grant, Lee, Patton, and so many others walked that glorious campus. You could almost feel their presence, and history lurked around every corner. The statue of Patton clutching binoculars stands near the library, for instance. The story one tour guide tells says that when the great general was questioned about why he took five years to graduate from West Point, Patton answered that he could never find the library. Having a sense of humor, Mrs. Patton suggested having his statue erected in front of the building.

Captivated: If you have ever had a magical evening, you know what I mean. We said our goodbyes to Matthew, then Hope, the Captain, and I stayed for a band concert at Trophy Point—the most scenic spot at West Point where the Hudson runs around Constitution Island. As the West Point jazz band played, what looked to be an ancient paddle-wheel boat tugged around the island while a train made its way around the mountain. The sun set, the band played, Hope fell asleep and the Captain and I took in the moment. Our son was now a West Point cadet.

Grateful: Just, grateful.

✳ ONE HOLIDAY AT A TIME

A faithful man will abound with blessings, but he
who hastens to be rich will not go unpunished.

PROVERBS 28:20

I remember the year my five daughters and I went to the grocery store together to conquer the Thanksgiving shopping. In past years it had been my oldest daughter, Bethany, and me, but the mission had outgrown us—it took all the girls and Mom Dot, too.

I love everything about Thanksgiving. I loved it when my son Matthew texted me from West Point that he was finally on the bus. I loved the thought of him taking the seven hour bus trip to join us for Thanksgiving, especially the year he saw our Virginia home for the first time. The kids made a sign to surprise him.

Traditions are still important to my children, and after the Thanksgiving feast, we begin the familiar Christmas rituals. From shopping on Black Friday to Christmas Eve Open House or Talent Show, we savor each one.

All this tradition had me thinking of a chat I had one summer while we were still living in Florida. I sat down at the picnic table with new baby Hope while Captain Fun took a walk with the kids at one of our favorite seaside parks. It just so happened that the Treasure Coast Atheists were having a picnic at the pavilion that day. An older gentleman beside me struck up a conversation, and I could see by his name tag that he was part of the group.

As we chatted, I learned he was from Vermont, one of my favorite places on earth. The conversation found its way to the topic of faith, and I shared with him that I was a Christian.

That's when he said something that I haven't forgotten. "You know, most Christians think it was when prayer was taken out of schools that the demise of this country began, but I beg to differ."

Here I had to tell him that one of the first prayers I knew as a kid was The Lord's Prayer, and guess where I learned it? Public school. He thought that was interesting.

"I think," he continued, "the real break down of the family began when stores started opening on Sundays and families stopped saving that day just to be together. Folks got too busy for the family."

Like I said, I am grateful our principal led us in The Lord's Prayer every morning, but his point was valid. I couldn't help but think about how many stores were opting to open their doors on Thanks-giving Day. Maybe families would make it a tradition to shop together, with the focus being on gratitude that they were blessed to be able to do so. But maybe not.

One thing is for sure, though. The Sims family will always be at home, sitting around the Thanksgiving table, each of us saying why we are thankful. Captain Fun will announce that it's time for the annual Sims Family Football Game. Dorothy will do cheers on the sideline. I will hold the baby. (I *always* hold the baby.) Mom Dot will watch if it's not too cold.

Families have the freedom to observe Thanksgiving any way they want—around the dinner table or at the mall. But I do hope with this invisible barrier that's been broken, we won't eventually skip Thanksgiving altogether.

Let's keep the focus on counting our blessings, one holiday at a time.

FULL

*I am the Lord your God, who brought you out of the land
of Egypt; Open your mouth wide, and I will fill it.*

PSALM 81:10

I cannot imagine the laundry you must do.

Your grocery bill must rival your mortgage.

Do you *all* go on vacation? *Together?*

How will you put all those kids through college?

When do you have time to yourself?

When do you and your husband ever manage time together?

Did all those children come out of *your* body?

Are all those children yours *and* his?

Are you this child's mother? (Referring to Hope—I am often mistaken as her grandmother. Oh, joy.)

How big of a turkey do you have to buy?

Christmas must be something at your house.

And, my favorite: You have your hands full.

Yes, my hands *are* full. As is my sink, the washer, the dryer, every clothes hamper, every bedroom, every bed, my twelve-passenger van, and every chair at my Thanksgiving table.

I suspect this is just the tip of the iceberg—contrary to popular belief, the grandkids aren't here yet. Some of the kids tease the Captain and me, saying they are all going to have ten kids so we will have one hundred grandchildren.

Bring them on, I say. I am liking the thought of this Thanks-living theme.

The Captain and I are, indeed, full: Full house, full hands, full table, full hearts.

What more can a family ask for?

THIRTEEN REASONS ✦ TO BE THANKFUL

Blessed is everyone who fears the Lord, who walks in His ways. When you eat the labor of your hands, you shall be happy, and it shall be well with you. Your wife shall be like a fruitful vine in the very heart of your house. Your children like olive plants all around your table. Behold, thus shall the man be blessed who fears the Lord.

PSALM 128: 1-4

Another Thanksgiving meal was over, but I couldn't let the day slip by without expressing my gratitude. "I'm thankful that I have more kids than can fit around this table," I said. It's true, isn't it? Every year we are deeply grateful for the ones we love the most.

I love to document things, and one particular Thanksgiving I set out to write a list of "Top Ten Reasons to Be Thankful." Under the circumstances, I had to stretch it a bit.

1. Robert (aka Captain Fun). The summer of my 19th year, a (very) few guys showed up at my door to take me out every now and then. When Robert didn't appear for a while, my dad spoke up at dinner one night. "Whatever happened to Robert?" he said. "He was the only one I ever liked." My feelings exactly.

2. Mom Dot. She buys KFC every Sunday after church and McDonald's every Saturday night so the Captain and I can go out. (You need that, she says. She's right.) She would fund a fast food Thanksgiving if I would allow it, yet the dog took more medicine than she did, even at 87.

3. Rob (aka Tiger). My oldest—the one with whom I grew up. A reader, a writer, full of smarts and a role model to his nine siblings, even though the younger ones barely know him (he and Hope are nearly 25 years apart, after all). Married to

Becky, in graduate school that year for aviation at University of North Dakota where, they both admitted, it was even colder than Vermont.

4. Becky. So thankful for this woman who married my firstborn. She is industrious, frugal, creative and a minimalist blogger. When she joined our family, she gained four new brothers and five new sisters, and she embraced them all so beautifully.

5. Bethany. My oldest daughter—we grew up together, too. Poise, grace, tiny in stature (half of her siblings tower over her and the other half eventually will), and was graduate school bound that year. Sister of the year. Volunteer of the year—she taught Sunday school, coordinated Upward cheer-leading, and sang the National Anthem at the Richmond St Jude Thanksgiving walk. (Did I mention she sings like an angel?)

6. Matthew. A poet and musician who observes everything around him. Every time Matthew came in from West Point, I ached for my parents to see it, to know it, even to visit that awesome campus with us. The best way to describe Matt? "A watched pot never boils," I once said when he was not yet a teen. "But a neglected one boils over,"

he replied. Mom Dot tells me I will never find the end of that boy.

7. Ben. Outgoing. Fun. Diligent. Wired for work. Whether it's taking out the trash or cutting the grass, he really doesn't mind. In fact, he loves to work. He was set to graduate the following Spring and was ready to get on with it. Mom Dot said in her next life she wants to be Ben. Oh, and he has perfect teeth, too. (The dentist said so himself.)

8. Mary. Mary is a server. Whether it's dishes, cleaning, or changing a diaper, she sees what needs to be done and does it. She swims, she runs, she flies over hurdles on the track team, and she effortlessly puts out an impressive number of chin ups, too.

9. Emma. She runs. And runs. And runs. A disciplined cross-country runner, I often find Emma and five or six siblings on the den floor doing her core workout. Captain Fun joins them when he's home. (I hide on the stairs until they are done). What kind of sister is she? Around the Thanksgiving table when we said what we were thankful for, Dorothy simply said, "Emma."

10. Cory. Even though Cory was about to turn thirteen, Hope could still turn him into mush. He has a quick wit and a great sense of humor (he once wore a chicken suit to school). One day you might just turn your television on and see SIMS on the back of a pro jersey. Okay, I know every mother thinks that. But as one of his coaches said, that boy is a natural.

11. Dorothy. She takes up for the underdog, values her friends, and has endless patience with baby sister, Hope. Mom Dot says she was born to perform. I agree. In fact, I don't know how much longer I can resist putting Dorothy on YouTube singing some song with her jazzy alto voice. I apologize ahead of time.

12. Silas. Sid the Science Kid or maybe my absent-minded professor. One night around the dinner table, Captain Fun told a tale of his mischief with Bunsen burners in chemistry class. Silas was taking notes. I could see the wheels turning. Stay tuned.

13. Hope. My bonus baby—she is everybody's baby. She was almost two when this list was written, and since everyone was raising her, I am really only partially responsible for how she turns out.

When I tell folks how many people live in my house, they often respond, "You've got your hands full!"

Full. I love that word. My hands are full. Right this minute my stomach is full. My house is full, as is my laundry basket, my sink, and my lap most of the time. But most of all, my heart is full.

Hope your heart is full, too.

 A DAY IN THE LIFE

This is the day the Lord has made;
We will rejoice and be glad in it.

PSALM 118:24

When folks find out I have ten kids, the inevitable question is, "How do you do it all?" My reply is always the same. I could never do it all, so I just stick to the important stuff. When Hope was thirteen months and the oldest at home was a senior in high school, I took note of what a typical day looked like. It went something like this:

5:00 A.M. — The baby slept all night so I woke up before the alarm, grateful for an hour of quiet before anyone stirred. I flipped on the fireplace and the coffee pot and settled in for my daily dose of prayer and scripture.

6:30-9:00 A.M. — I sent three pairs of kids off to three different schools. Because half of my kids had sports after school, I left a simple but hot breakfast on the stove. Then it was on to lunches, where the sandwich assembly line resembled a game of solitaire. After I walked my youngest kids to the bus stop at 9:00, I chatted with the other moms, loving their unhurried pace. If weather permitted, I took the baby for a walk—the only workout I could fit into my life.

10:00 A.M. — I am not a meticulous housekeeper, but the kids gained on me if I didn't tidy up. I was soon over the housework and stopped to play with Hope. Since she was my late in life surprise, admittedly, I was about half grandma with this one.

11:00 A.M. — Hope watched

"Barney Goes to the Zoo" in her high chair while she ate lunch. The same show every day, but she would watch the whole episode, interacting with the animals. I was delighted she could be contained for forty-five minutes.

12:00 P.M. — Bath time. Hope played with her rubber duck family and tried to drink the tub water. (Now I know where the "Miss Lucy" song got its inspiration.) After her bath I rocked her until she dozed off, finding it easy to take the time to feel the moment before slipping her into bed.

1:00-3:00 P.M. — No matter how full the sink, the hamper, or the "to do" list, I rested, wrote and recharged until the baby woke up. Calls from the Captain or my son at the USMA were the only exceptions. My son often called midday, and I loved hearing about life at West Point and grew nostalgic thinking of how proud my parents would be.

3:20-4:15 P.M. — Six kids returned from school. Younger kids rode the bus home, but I had to pick up my athletes. Since I was the only driver, I did a lot of running, and I was counting the days until the next one got a driver's license. I was thankful I usually had someone to watch Hope so I didn't often have a crying baby in the car seat—about the only thing that still got under my skin after twenty-five years of babies.

4:00-6:00 P.M. — Homework and dinner. Mom Dot, my eighty-six year old mother-in-law, lived with us and was a tremendous help with homework and quizzing the kids on their various subjects. Four kids took a half hour "Hope shift," which gave me two hours to tidy up again and cook dinner, always while listening to Sinatra. I called on whoever was around to set the table, joking with the kids that I knew where they were hiding.

6:00-7:00 P.M. — Dinner and dishes. It was challenging to wait until 6:00 to serve (in my mind, dinner must be conquered), but family dinner time was a priority. I waited for my deserving husband—he was the breadwinner, after all—and my recent college graduate, Bethany, to get home from work. Eleven people around the table brought a lot of chatter, and I couldn't help but smile when one of them raised a hand for a turn to talk. Silas said something about kindergarten and Mom Dot mistook it for the Pentagon. "Being half-deaf makes life interesting," she said with a laugh. Someone checked the calendar to announce whether it was boys' night or girls' night to help with dishes.

7:30 P.M. — Hope to bed. I loved listening to the quiet as I rocked the baby one more time.

8:00-9:00 P.M. — Somewhere in this hour we had family devotions (complete with some wriggles and giggles). The time of connecting every night is vital to family health and I am quick to give credit to Captain Fun for starting this tradition. Afterwards, the younger ones went to bed while the older ones finished up homework.

9:00 P.M. — I saw my oldest son on the caller ID and eagerly answered. Having recently relocated to North Dakota to pursue a Master's in aviation, he reported he and his sweet wife like their new surroundings even though the high was 4 and the low was -14. I enjoyed talking with my oldest and found it hard to believe he was a grown, married man.

10:00 P.M. — Fell into bed knowing I would be doing—and loving—the important stuff all over again tomorrow.

FOR THE FATHER OF TEN ✴

And these words which I command you today shall be in your heart. You shall teach them diligently to your children, and shall talk of them when you sit in your house, when you walk by the way, when you lie down, and when you rise up. You shall bind them as a sign on your hand, and they shall be as frontlets between your eyes. You shall write them on the doorposts of your house and on your gates.

DEUTERONOMY 6:7-9

*I*t goes without saying that my husband, aka Captain Fun, deserves a tribute every Father's Day. It's hard to find a man who will go along with having ten kids. But from the beginning, it was no secret that I wanted a brood, and from the beginning, he has been on board.

Children are a blessing, a gift, a reward according to Psalm 127. But some would say that children are also expensive, messy, and a lot of work.

Enter Captain Fun. He is, first of all, fun, which I am not. While I try and keep a sense of humor by finding the funny in life with ten kids, he really is the one who finds the fun. One Father's Day weekend, for instance, we grilled out, watched two movies, went to the beach, and visited the pool—twice—in a span of forty-eight hours.

So many men would rather be on the golf course or out of town, away from their families, Mom Dot often says. But not Captain Fun. He is a hands-on, all-in dad who tries to cram in as much fun in a short amount of time as possible. We are all certain he holds the record for it.

Apart from his fun side, I love his ability to see things in our kids that I, or even they, sometimes cannot see. When Ben was undecided about the spring football season, his dad suggested he revisit lacrosse. Ben emerged from his JV season as MVP and walked onto the prep school team at West Point, scoring a hat trick in one of his first games.

He has told Matthew since he was a little boy that he possessed strong leadership qualities and even encouraged him to apply to the United States Military Academy. It wasn't easy, but his suspicions were confirmed. Matthew graduated from West Point and became an army officer.

When I was unsure about putting Silas in preschool, his dad thought it would be the right thing. He was right. Silas flourished in the school environment.

Though he goes by Captain Fun around here, I know the kids would agree he doesn't shy away from discipline. He makes integrity, hard work, and accountability the focus of fathering.

But my favorite thing about him is the way he gathers us every night for family devotions. He takes his time—but not too much time—exploring a passage of scripture, digging into it, putting a finger on where everyone is in their spiritual journey. Yet he stays transparent about his own walk of faith, too.

We talk a lot at our house about how popular the "point and laugh" trend is concerning men these days. This belittling is not good for men and not healthy for the psyche, I frequently remind my girls. It is especially not good for fathers.

Thank you, Captain Fun, for being the on board, all-in dad that you are. The kids and I are all the better because you are in our lives. You're fun. You're strong. You're kind. You're smart.

And you have made all the difference in our family.

WHAT I LIKE ABOUT YOU ✦

*Like arrows in the hands of a warrior, so
are the children of one's youth.*

PSALM 127:4

Our first born arrived on Easter Sunday, 1987, 10:56 P.M., eight pounds, eight ounces, twenty inches long. Because he was my first, I remember like it was yesterday. But what I recall just as clearly was when we broke the news to our families that he was on the way.

We had been married only a few months. Both my parents were still living, and family gatherings were frequent. No doubt these are the good ol' days, as referenced in an old favorite song of mine. We all gathered in a big circle at my sister's house, our plates in our laps. Captain Fun found a pause somewhere among all the conversations and said we had an announcement. Then he said it, which brought

gasps and applause from around the room. But what I most recall was Mom Dot throwing her arms up in the air like she had just won Heavyweight Champion of the World.

Not long after the baby arrived, she started calling him The Perfect One. Even though nine more came after him, she calls him that to this day.

I am the youngest of eight, and my dad named a racehorse after me when I was in fifth grade— Charming Margie. I think my siblings got it. I am the baby. Not the same as the favorite, but I held a special place in my dad's heart.

It's sort of the same thing with Mom Dot's first-born grandchild. Her husband had passed away the year before the Captain and I started dating. I never even got to meet him. Needless to say, she bemoans the fact that he missed out on all these grandkids, and they missed out on him. Tiger, as we call him, came along at a time when the view was dim from where she sat. The first grandchild after such a dark time of grief, he was and is and always will be The Perfect One.

In Sims birthday tradition, here's what I like about my first born. He survived my parenting back when I thought I knew what I was doing but I really didn't. (We grew up together, I often remind him.) I like the way he stays in touch with his siblings, even though Hope is 25 years younger. Why, he even suggested that sometime in the future we pick a central point and rent a house for a week. I love that about him. The list goes on: smart, in tune,

steady, intentional. An all-around great role model for his nine younger siblings. He lit up Mom Dot's life when he appeared on the scene all those years ago, and he still brings joy, fun, and adventure wherever he goes.

I can hardly believe that I only see my oldest son maybe once a year. For some reason when he was growing up, I never saw that coming. That's the thing about being a mom, isn't it? You go from caretaker to coach to counselor to comrade. Yet while it's all unfolding you don't see it until it is upon you and you've worked yourself out of a job.

While I don't see him as The Perfect One like his grandmother does, (that would never do), I don't tell him often enough how absolutely perfect he is at being the oldest.

MEET MOM DOT ✳

I thank God, whom I serve with a pure conscience, as my
forefathers did, as without ceasing I remember you in my prayers
night and day, greatly desiring to see you, being mindful of your
tears, that I may be filled with joy, when I call to remembrance the
genuine faith that is in you, which dwelt first in your grandmother
Lois and your mother Eunice, and I am persuaded is in you also.

2 TIMOTHY 1:3-6

There are two kinds of grandparents; the lonely and the tired. Meet Mom Dot, who is part of the latter group.

Captain Fun and I married when we were just twenty and twenty-one, and Mom Dot gave me her stamp of approval right from the start. I'd had my eye on him for over a year, in fact, and it was at her suggestion that he finally called and asked me out. I owe her for that one.

I remember when we found out we were expecting our first child a few months after we were married. Still a new bride, I was a little nervous about what everyone would say about us starting a family so soon. We had all gathered at my sister's for Labor Day when the Captain and I announced we had a little announcement. Mom Dot did not hold back. She has told me many times over the years, in fact, that the grandkids brought the sunshine back into her life after the death of her husband two years prior.

In Sims' family tradition, we gathered around the lunch table on her birthday to say "What We Like About You." The list was long: comfort, affirmation, generosity, energy, and the way she never fails to ask how everybody's day was. And always her sense of humor. I know of no one else, for instance, who deliberately put the wrong year on their head stone. "I only made myself one year younger," she scolds herself. "I should have taken off five or ten years!"

"You're a fierce grandmother," I said when it was my turn, to which all the kids agreed. Coaches be warned if you don't give one of the grandkids enough playing time. Mom Dot will be at the game, and she'll be watching. My list goes on: she buys all the chips, treats the kids to McDonald's every Saturday night so Captain Fun and I can go out to dinner, and folds all the laundry—including matching socks for twenty feet. "And I love the way you pray," I added. (I should note that this list is *not* in the order of importance.)

The Captain said she was always the favorite mom in the neighborhood when he was growing up. When one of our kids complimented him on his vocabulary, he reminded them who raised him.

Mom Dot would not tell this, so I will—she scored on the Mensa level on the IQ test years ago. Even now she can still quote lengthy passages from Shakespeare.

After everyone was finished, she had a thing or two to say. "I love all the compliments, but just look, just look at my grandkids." Here she paused and gestured around the table. "I have the most wonderful, best-looking grandkids in the world and it is an easy task to love all of you," she said, adding that there was so much love around our dinner table. "I believe I could sell my seat."

If every grandparent was like Mom Dot, there would only be one category of grandparents: the loved.

Thank you, Mom Dot, for loving your ten grandchildren so freely.

DADDY, THE HORSES AND ME ✦

Do you not know that those who run in a race all run, but only one receives the prize? Run in such a way that you may win.

I CORINTHIANS 9:24

Every year when March seventh rolls around, my thoughts turn to my dad. I was his baby of six girls and two boys. Little Marge is what he called me. To him, Little Marge is who I always was.

Some of my earliest memories are of getting up with him at sunrise and feeding the horses, dragging bales of hay that outweighed me across the yard, seeing mares give birth, or watching in horror as my dad untangled a horse from barbed wire.

When Secretariat won the Triple Crown in 1973, I was eight years old, and my dad tore a picture of him out of a magazine to put up on my wall. While other little girls wanted dolls and dresses for Christmas, I wanted boots and a cowboy hat or some new piece of tack for my horse.

Daddy loved every aspect of horses: caring for them, owning them, riding them, betting on them. I remember once when he was riding our mare Dolly she fell and rolled on him, breaking his ribs. It didn't stop him though, as he eventually got back on. Dolly's foal, Princess, was my horse. A princess in name only, she repeatedly tried to throw me. The boy next door laughed at me, but Daddy always told me to climb back into the saddle. One day, though, I guess he'd had enough of her antics, as I came home from school and learned that Princess had been sold. That's the way my dad did things.

By the time I was in fifth grade, we had ten horses that grazed right in our front yard. Every day when I got off the school bus, the horses would trot toward me. Those spirited thoroughbreds scared me to death, but I knew my friends were watching from the bus, so I resisted the urge to run. The young race horses are etched in my memory: Whiskey Harry, named after my great grandfather; Green Eyed Primp, named after my mother, and Charming Margie, named after— well, let's just say she gave my siblings more proof that I *was* the spoiled baby.

It was Daddy's dream to win the Kentucky Derby, the Belmont, the Preakness—the Triple Crown. Since horse racing was illegal in Tennessee, we moved to race our horses, and I became familiar with words like trifecta and handicapping. On the evenings we didn't go to the track, we sat on our back porch and listened to the races. I became very familiar with the announcer's call, "And they're off!" No matter the odds, my mother always bet her lucky numbers, two, five, and eight. Daddy teased her, saying the horses didn't know what number they were wearing.

Green Eyed Primp got us into the Winner's Circle once, but once was not enough in such a costly business, and we returned to Memphis where Daddy sold cars for a living. I have never forgotten how my dad had the courage to pursue his dream.

Alzheimer's took Daddy many years ago, but it cannot take what I learned from him. He was not a perfect man, but whether I failed a math test—and I failed many—or was thrown from a horse, his message was the same: get back up, he would say, reminding me that if it weren't for failure, success wouldn't mean anything.

I've got too much Baptist in me to ever bet on a horse, but I am forever grateful to have memories that most little girls only dream of. I will always cherish the memories of Daddy, the horses and me.

SOMEONE'S WATCHING YOU ✳

So then each of us shall give account of himself to God. Therefore,
let us not judge one another anymore, but rather resolve this, not
to put a stumbling block or a cause to fall in our brother's way.

ROMANS 14:12-13

My little guy, Silas, could so easily become a screen head. Whatever screen is on, be it the TV, Xbox, or computer, you better believe he is watching.

His big brother Cory was home sick one day and wanted some screen time on the computer. I told him okay—I make an exception to my "no screens" rule for a sick one—but just be sure Silas can't see it. Next thing I knew, Cory was in the recliner with a blanket over his head. His brother didn't even notice. Or so I thought.

"Can I have my Barney computer?" Silas asked me the next morning. For once, I actually remembered where something was, so I retrieved it for him. Next thing I knew, Silas was under his blanket, playing with his Barney computer.

You know where I am going with this, but I had to let Cory in on it. "Cory, look at Silas," I said. "He saw you under the blanket on the computer, so now he thinks that is what he is supposed to do."

"Can you imagine if Silas is over at a friend's and the friend wants to play computer?" Cory said. "Silas will say, 'Sure, do you have a blanket?'"

We had a good laugh.

The teachable moment was glaring. "Remember as you get older, Cory, that whatever Silas sees you do, he might do it, too." We chatted about it for a minute. I think he got it.

There's a teachable moment for

us parents as well. A reminder that as our kids grow up, they will do as we do.

We better believe it—they are watching.

GOT BEN?

That you also aspire to lead a quiet life, to mind your own business, and to work with your own hands, as we commanded you, that you may walk properly toward those who are outside and that you may lack nothing.

I THESSALONIANS 4:11-12

At our house, birthdays are pretty well set: we gather around for a favorite dish, cake, presents and the traditional "What I like about you."

Ben's birthday was approaching. What would I say? Ben is a workhorse. The year we pulled into Florida from New York with quite a caravan, it was Ben, in fact, who confirmed my suspicions that kids come with internal wiring. Ben was a trooper, though, spending his sixteenth birthday unloading the moving truck with his dad, who was less than Captain Fun on that day (even the Captain has an off day now and then). Nevertheless, Ben didn't complain too much.

When Ben was eight, he had his tonsils out. It was a tough, painful recovery. "Help me" he scribbled on a piece of paper when he woke up and saw the Captain and me standing by his bed, adding, "I want to go home, please" a few minutes later. I believe I still have that piece of paper somewhere in a memory box.

We took him home and got him comfortable on the couch with, *ahem*, all the video games and Popsicles a kid could hold. After forty-eight hours of recovery, he got up and started cleaning the den. "What are you doing?" I asked.

"It's a mess in here," he replied in a hoarse whisper. A true statement, but with a post-op boy, his three older siblings, and his younger siblings being six, five, three, and (as Loretta Lynn sings) one on the way,

I was doing the best I could. Nevertheless, Ben cleaned the room until I made him lie down again.

When he was twelve, he inherited the chore of cutting the grass. Older brother Matthew had held the job for a good three years and gladly passed the lawn mowing down. Ben relished the first time he got to cut the grass—and the second, and the third. Even when we lived in upstate New York and he had acres and acres to mow, I could still hear him celebrating as he rode on the mower, singing loudly with his ear phones in place.

Ben's middle name is initiative. At the beach he helped his dad haul umbrellas, chairs, and towels for ten—without being asked. At home, when it was boys night to do the dishes, the joke was you better eat fast because Ben will take your plate before you're done.

His greatest flaw? He has to be fed. Mounds of food. Several times a day. Every day. "There's the woman I love," he'd joke repeatedly when he came home from his daily summer football workout. "Only because I feed you," I'd laugh, and he'd agree.

What happens when I didn't feed him? You don't want to know, but I will tell you. Familiar with Dr. Jekyll and Mr. Hyde? The Hulk? Gorillas in the Mist? *That's* what happened. He was in seventh grade when we discovered his tendency toward low blood sugar, and it took the whole school year to pinpoint it. It didn't dawn on us until the very end of his basketball season, as almost every game he would shut down with an Eeyore-like cloud over his head. Then we started feeding him right before the games. He hasn't been the same since.

But when he eats on time, he is in tune with everything around him. "You okay?" he often asks me out of the blue.

"Be sure and write about his high voltage smile," Mom Dot said, adding that as long as you've got Ben, you've got all the help you need. In fact, Mom Dot likes to make up bumper stickers. "Here's one for ya," she said a few years ago when Ben was being his usual helpful self. "*Got Ben?*"

Yes, we've got Ben. And we are sure glad we do.

ME, SICK?

So then, my beloved brethren, let every man be swift to
hear, slow to speak, slow to wrath; for the wrath of man
does not produce the righteousness of God.

JAMES 1:19-20

I started feeling a familiar pain in my lower back. Kidney stone, I self-diagnosed, as I'd had one about twenty-five years earlier. Over the years, it had surfaced here and there, but if I drank lots of water it worked its way out.

This time aspirin didn't help. Ibuprofen didn't touch it. Late into the night, the Captain noticed I was a little restless. "You okay?"

"Yes. Kidney stone. I need to drink more water," I said. "And would you rub my back?" He brought me two more pain pills and rubbed my back. I finally fell asleep.

The next morning, the pain was still present—a dull ache with a little burn mixed in. But, again, I knew that pain. Kidney stones. I resolved I would drink gallons of water and get rid of this thing.

The snow had started falling, along with the temperature. Try as I might, I couldn't shake it. I started to feel funny. Maybe I was running a fever.

102.5

"How about I take you to the doctor?" the Captain said.

"Oh, no, I know this pain. I just need to drink more water." Besides, I had heard the temperature outside was nine degrees. Way too cold to get out with a fever.

Eight inches of snow fell that day. Come Sunday, church was canceled—not that I was going anyway. My fever held on at 102.7. "I found a home test for UTIs," the Captain said. "I am going to get it for you. If it's positive, I am taking you to the emergency room."

Yes, sir.

He did. It was. I felt like a noodle. I looked like death. But I kept my end of the deal and braved the cold.

Two IV's and four blood draws later, the ER doc came in with his diagnosis.

"You're dehydrated."

But I drank all that water.

"Your fever is 103."

Oh.

"Your heart is racing."

"My heart's not racing," I protested.

"Your heart rate is 130," he said.

Ah.

"And your white count is elevated," he continued down the list of symptoms. "I am sending you for a CT scan. We might admit you." With that he left.

"I will be very surprised if they admit me," I said to my nurse, who didn't reply.

About an hour after the scan, the doctor returned.

"You have two kidney stones, one of which is blocking your kidney, causing a kidney infection. I am admitting you. You will probably be here a few days."

I glanced at the Captain, who had a knowing look.

The doctor wasn't finished. "If I just put you on antibiotics, you will not get well. You need to have surgery immediately to drain the infec-tion. The surgeon will be in to see you soon. The stones can be treated later."

I thanked him, and he left. Then I knew there was someone else I had to thank. "Thanks for bringing me in," I said to the Captain, meaning it. "And next time I won't resist."

"You're my wife. I love you—I want you to be healthy," he answered with a gentle pat on my pin-cushiony arm.

"Well, I'm glad you have the same standard for yourself as you do for your kids," my oldest son chuckled on the phone when I told him the story. I admit, it's true. I am not one to dash off to the emergency room, no matter who is sick.

The whole episode was a gentle reminder of what marriage is for—to help each other, love each other, listen to each other. Believe it or not, there have been other times when I didn't get it (remember when the house was on fire?). And—I know this comes as no surprise—this episode was a reminder of what an attentive, cheerful caregiver my husband, a.k.a. Captain Fun, is. Thank you, Captain, for watching out for me.

As for me, I have also learned how fast you can get seriously ill, and I've resolved to be quicker to listen to my spouse.

Maybe every marriage could benefit from that.

REMEMBERING MY MOM

Let your father and your mother be glad,
and let her who bore you rejoice.
PROVERBS 23:25

"Losing your mom is harder than you think it is going to be," I reminded my friend, still raw from the loss of her own mom.

"You've got that right," she agreed.

There is a certain time of year that always gets to me—when spring is in the air, and the anniversary of my mother's death approaches. I will simply never forget her and all she meant to me.

In my mind, I see her in the moon as it rises above the rooftops across the street. I cannot see a full moon without thinking of her. Maybe my memory deceives me (perhaps it was a dream?), but I remember my mom showing me a poem she had written about the full moon peering through the trees. Now a writer my-self, I secretly hope I will discover it one day in some random box.

I see her in the ocean waves. Oh, how she loved the ocean. When I was living exactly four miles from Mobile Bay, I knew she would happily, blissfully move in if she were still alive.

I see her every time a seagull flies overhead. I chuckle as I recall the time I came out of a beach bathroom as a kid and walked right into a flock. Consequently, they cut loose as they flew over me, bathing me in bird droppings. "Good luck!" my mother insisted. To which I replied, "If that is good luck, then what is bad luck?"

I see her every time one of my kids opens an umbrella in the house, hangs up the calendar before

171

January first, or a black cat crosses my path. "Bad luck. Bad luck. Turn around!" she used to insist.

I see her on her birthday, which we shared. It took me years to get used to celebrating without her.

The list is lengthy for all of us who have lost our moms, isn't it?

Beach hats, *I Love Lucy*, lucky numbers (2-5-8), cheesy Sinatra movies, "Red Sails in the Sunset" by Nat Cole, and the orange haired angel ornament she gave me when I was little "because you're my red headed angel." I still have it.

But losing your mother, tough as it is, is simply a part of life. I am grateful to have had her for thirty-seven years, as I went to school with a couple of kids who had already lost their moms. I simply don't know how they managed.

I will take Dr. Seuss's advice and smile because of the years I did have. I celebrate her every day because of the things she left me:

Atmosphere, atmosphere, atmosphere. It's why I play Sinatra, Michael Buble, Ella Fitzgerald, and Tony Bennett. Every. Single. Day. While I am cooking dinner.

No tolerance for sass. This is the biggest favor she ever did me—modeling no tolerance for sass from her eight kids as now I am the mom of ten.

Warning me ahead of time. "You never quit missing your mother," she told me after I inquired as a kid if she still missed her mother, who died when I was six. Her words have come back to me many times, even released me from the unrealistic expectation of ever fully recovering now that she is gone.

I love you, Mom. I miss you. And, Mom, I can't thank you enough.

JUBILEE

For you did not receive the spirit of bondage again to
fear, but you received the spirit of adoption by whom
we cry out, 'Abba, Father.' The Spirit Himself bears
witness with our spirit that we are children of God.

ROMANS 8:15-1

The day Jubilee Kate arrived and we became Gigi and Grandad was an unforgettable day for the Captain and me.

Our son, Matt and his wife, Melissa announced about eighteen months prior that they were going to adopt before they attempted to have biological children. They wanted it that way so their first one would know that he or she was chosen.

Matt is in the military and wouldn't have to pay a red cent for a biological birth. Instead, he and Melissa chose to tackle the mountain of money and the mountain of paperwork required. Within three weeks of their file going active, they were chosen.

The birth mom looked through the files at the adoption agency and knew immediately that Matt and Melissa were the right parents for her unborn baby. When they got the word that they had been matched, they were ecstatic. When they called to tell us, we celebrated— from Mom Dot who would become a great grandmother at ninety-one, right down to Hope, who became Aunt Hope at the ripe old age of six.

As they suspected, Matt would be deployed by the time the baby arrived. Was it possible for me to come and be with Melissa? Well, of course. I could not wait to get my hands on that baby. It had been six whole years since I had one of my own. That was a long time for me.

We were visiting Memphis and in my sister's pool when Melissa reached Robert with the news that the birth mother had gone into labor. He was taking Mom Dot to visit their old stomping grounds but hurried back to my sister's and got us out of the pool. Never has our big family packed up and rushed home so quickly.

The next day, the Captain (God bless him) put me on a plane for Texas. After many delays, I landed well after midnight. The sister of a West Point classmate of Matt's (God bless her) picked me up and drove me to the hospital. Don't worry, Jubilee, Gigi is coming!

The hospital had provided Melissa with a bed and Jubilee was rooming in with her. There she was, all 6 pounds of her, fuzzy black hair and the tiniest legs I had ever seen. The labor was 24-plus hours and Melissa had been with the birth mom every step of the way. Would I take the 5:00 A.M. feeding? Um, I think I can do that.

Next morning, I met the birth mother. Not yet thirty, beautiful and brave, with a quick wit and easy laugh. Throughout our forty-eight hour stay at the hospital, the birth mom requested to spend time with Jubilee. It was an open adoption, and I confess this made me nervous every time she asked to see her. Would she change her mind? But each time we entered the room, she presented Melissa with a gift for Ju-

bilee. A bright yellow dress; a letter to her ("You will always be my first child," she wrote); pictures of herself growing up so Jubilee could see if she looked like her birth mom.

I met the birth mom's aunt, her best friend, other family, who all applauded the choice she made to place Jubilee for adoption. The social worker commented that she had never seen an adoption that had such support on both sides.

On the day she signed the papers relinquishing her rights, I was standing in the hallway as she exited the room. She was crying, and I grabbed her and hugged her. "I will never forget this day, and I will never forget what you did," I said. She offered a smile and walked out the door.

I know babies. I've had ten of them. But this adoption journey was a new experience for me. I didn't completely get it until it all unfolded. I have had ten babies who were 100% covered by prayer (every mother's prayer: please let it be healthy) and 80% covered by insurance. Matt and Melissa joyfully raised the aforementioned mountain of money to adopt a baby they knew may not be healthy (though, thankfully, she was).

What a picture of what God does for us. What a picture of the beauty of adoption.

Section Four:
FRIENDS

My husband always says that friendship is one of the greatest gifts we can give our children. Sometimes it happens effortlessly; other times you have to keep trying. Either way (while keeping an eye out for bad influences, of course), let your kids know that friends aren't optional. While you're at it, remember it for yourself, too. We need each other.

PASSING IT ON ✴

And we urge you, brethren, to recognize those who labor among you, and are over you in the Lord and admonish you, and to esteem them very highly in love for their work's sake. Be at peace among yourselves.

1 THESSALONIANS 5:12-13

The older I get, the more I realize there are folks who have invested in my life whom I know I could never repay.

When my new best friend, Pan (don't dare call her "Pam"), invited me to church where her daddy was the preacher, I went. As far as I remember, the first time I heard him share the Gospel, I committed my life to Christ. It didn't matter that I was only nine and didn't fully understand. I knew I needed forgiveness, and Brother Jackson told me where to find it.

Almost every weekend I could be found at Pan's house. I remember hearing her mother's lovely soprano voice as I sat beside her in the church pew, not to mention the dozens of times she shushed two giggly young girls. After Sunday service it was off to her house for lunch where something delicious simmered in the crock pot.

The Jackson family read a scripture before every meal, and because I was a guest, I often got the honor. I don't remember what the verse said on that particular Sunday, but I will never forget pronouncing "Psalms"—a word I'd never seen before—as "P-salms" with full emphasis on the *P*. Mrs. Jackson, of course, remained composed. Pan thought it was hilarious, but all Brother Jackson had to do was raise a bushy eyebrow to silence her. I have often wondered if he, too, had to contain his laughter.

Because of the Jackson family, I

was in church "every time the door was open," as my mother used to say. Sunday school, service, and puppet team year-round; VBS and Camp Good News every summer. The songs, the stories, the teaching, and the preaching are all still with me.

Then there is Brother Mark, my youth pastor from middle and high school. With his preaching aimed directly at the teenage heart, he addressed topics I had never heard before like, "How to Raise Your Parents."

Brother Mark's approach to dating was also new to me. "God has someone picked out just for you," he told our group of wide-eyed girls. "Make a list of what you want in your husband, and don't settle for anything less." Good thing I listened. How else could I have found a man who was willing to have and provide for ten kids?

Finally, my college pastor, Heldur (yes, that's his real name), welcomed me into my first church as a grown up, taught me how to freely worship, and led one of the most tightly knit group of young adults of which I have ever been a part. Even when we had a group reunion, he effortlessly brought us back togeth-er, picking up right where we had left off.

About five kids into being a mom, I knew I was in over my head. Enter Jean Stockdale, a mentor under whose teaching I sat for nine years in a Bible study that was simply called MOMS. Week after week, Jean taught me (and two hundred of my closest friends) parenting principles that I didn't even know I needed.

Because I am a mom, I often reflect on the precious people who influenced me during those years. I have tried to swing my doors wide open to my kids' friends like the Jacksons did for me. I want so much to make Christ real and relevant not only to my own teenagers but to their friends as well. As my kids have worked to navigate the current culture and then leave the launch pad, I have prayed for God to send folks like Brother Mark, Heldur, and Jean into their lives.

To those folks along the way, I say thanks. Thanks for taking the time to invest in me. The way you spoke into my life when I was young has stuck with me, changed me, and sustained me.

I know I can never repay you except by passing it on.

NOW I KNOW ✦

*The Lord is my shepherd; I shall not want. He makes
me lie down in green pastures; He leads me beside
the still waters. He restores my soul; He leads me in
the paths of righteousness for His name's sake.*

PSALM 23:1-2

"**A** company in Vermont wants to interview me," my husband said to me one Spring day.

"Vermont?" I said. "I don't want to move to Vermont."

Oh, but I did. I just didn't know it.

"Lord," I prayed, telling Him something He already knew, "Robert is in Vermont on a job interview. But we're not moving to Vermont."

Oh, but we were. I just didn't know it.

"Honey? Guess what?" he said through the phone. "We're moving to Vermont!"

I hung up the phone, excited, then scared. Could a family with eight kids move from Memphis to Vermont? I wasn't sure.

But we could. And we did. Eight kids from six weeks old to seventeen years.

Surely those sophisticated New Englanders will think I talk funny, not to mention too much, I thought to myself. Did they even wear makeup in Vermont?

I very quickly saw I could not have been more wrong. They thought my southern ways endearing, even calling my twangy accent *charming*, and they didn't even mind my lipstick.

It was forty-two degrees when we pulled in on June 2, 2004. "If it's that cold in June," my sister pondered, "what is January like?" I was afraid of the answer.

But Vermonters embraced the cold summers. For the rest of that summer, in fact, I kept waiting for it to warm up, for summer to really arrive. At the community pool I wrapped a towel around baby Dorothy to shield her from the cold—in July. The lifeguards wore sweatshirts over their bathing suits. The kids' lips turned blue in the pool. Even in August, the pavement was cool to my feet.

"Oh, the humidity!" the Vermonters would wail when the temps would approach 90 cool degrees for a day (or a minute) or two in August.

"You don't know anything about humidity," I told them.

"And you don't know anything about the cold," they answered. They were right about that.

Vermont did teach me about the cold, yes. But it taught me so much more. I was taken aback by their hospitality—something we southerners are known for. Their work ethic, their frugality, their loyalty, and I can't forget their good stewardship. Would you believe that the apples in the school lunch were grown at the local orchard?

"People are so accepting here,"

my oldest son observed upon arriving home from school that first week. We had moved his senior year—usually a challenging time to change schools. Another needless worry; for him the move was seamless. In fact, he met his wife in English class and married her a few years later.

I was delighted when the teenage girls from school rang the doorbell to invite my then fifteen-year-old Bethany to come along with them on a Sunday afternoon. But they weren't going to the mall, not these Vermont girls. They were going to hike a mountain.

Upon a recent visit to Vermont, I was filled with nostalgia and gratitude as Lake Champlain came into view. I pointed out the cows to the kids and was once again charmed by the covered bridges, smitten with the overall loveliness of the place. Though lots of folks visit Vermont for the beauty, it is the people that keep me coming back. What a gift, a privilege, a blessing.

Thank you, Vermont. Now I know.

WHAT FRIENDS ARE FOR ✦

*Now when he had finished speaking to Saul, the
soul of Jonathan was knit to the soul of David, and
Jonathan loved him as his own soul.*

I SAMUEL 18:1

A visit to Vermont had me thinking about friendship. Friends come in all varieties, and I have decided I need every kind.

With some friends you can pick up right where you left off. You don't see each other often or contact each other much, but it doesn't matter—they listen as if no time has passed.

Then there are friends who build you up by their presence. Encouragement seeps from every pore. I encountered many during my visit, and they always leave me feeling like I've had an energy drink.

I've had a few friends in my lifetime who slip in quietly at my hour of need and help me in a way that leaves me speechless. When my mother died after a long bout with cancer, for instance, my phone rang the morning of her funeral. It was my friend and neighbor, Angela. "Get out the clothes your kids are wearing to the funeral. I am coming to pick them up and iron them. Then I will bring them back." I didn't even argue. I just obeyed.

A few minutes later, the doorbell rang. She slipped in, offered a hug, took the clothes, and left. She knew me well enough to know that I would pull out the crumpled clothes for seven kids that day and be reduced to tears. It was one of the kindest things anyone has ever done for me, and I will never forget it.

There are some people who say, "Let me know if I can do anything." Then there are others, like Angela, who do it.

181

I need every type of friend. But I also want to *be* every type of friend—the energizer, the doer, the listener. The friend who will get past the awkwardness of the moment and simply offer a helping hand, a listening ear, a presence.

Now *that's* what friends are for.

BIRTHDAY PARTIES ✦

A man who has friends must show himself friendly,
but there is a friend who sticks closer than a brother.
PROVERBS 18:24

When I reached the point of six kids still at home, birthday party invitations averaged about one a week at my house. I even headed out in a snowstorm to, you guessed it, a birthday bash for a classmate of Silas's.

When I was a younger mom, I admit I would let the event slide right by, never making a serious attempt to get my kids to them. Sometimes I called with regrets without even checking the calendar. Too much trouble, too much time, too much expense. I could always find a reason.

But somewhere along the way, I began to tune in to the importance of these play dates. I realized birthday parties were great occasions for my kids to connect with classmates in a setting other than school. While I was not naive as to what can go on at middle school parties, I did make an effort to find out if the setting is acceptable. (I am one of those annoying moms who calls and asks suspicious questions: Will parents be home? Will the kids be supervised? What movies will you watch?) It was worth the trouble, as one of my kids was on the shy side in middle school, and it was at a birthday party that he entered into a fun friendship.

I even learned to turn shopping for gifts into a hobby—scaling clearance aisles, stashing paper, tape, and those handy birthday bags. For a while I was having trouble keeping up with my finds, until I struck up a conversation with a lady in line (remember, I am a chatty southerner). When I shared with her how I loved to shop ahead for birthday parties but sometimes had trouble finding my bargains at home, she suggested I keep everything in a "gift closet."

Thank you, chatty shopping lady, for that good advice.

Although my Saturdays were often busy with birthday parties, I figured...who knows, I just might make a new friend, too.

THE JACOBI HOUSE ✸

And if it seems evil to you to serve the Lord, choose for yourselves this day whom you will serve, whether the gods which your fathers served that were on the other side of the River, or the gods of the Amorites, in whose land you dwell. But as for me and my house, we will serve the Lord.

JOSHUA 24:15

I have never minded moving. I like change and what it brings—new places, new people, new experiences.

When we left our house in New York, however, I confess, I wished I could take the house with me. From the view, to the library, to the platter cabinet in the sideboard, I loved everything about it. But especially the history.

"Dr. Jacobi delivered me," a repairman told me when he came to fix my dishwasher.

"I remember that tree," said a new acquaintance who had come to pick me up for dinner when we first moved to Norwich. "When I was a little girl and Dr. Jacobi turned on that tree, I knew the Christmas season had started," she said, nostalgia in her voice.

I pointed. "If you look closely, you can still see lights dangling from the top branches."

Yet another repairman visited and proclaimed that Dr. Jacobi had delivered him, as well. "I was named after him."

Everywhere I went in Norwich, I meet people who were touched by the life of Dr. Martin Jacobi. Born in Germany, Jacobi could see what was coming with Hitler's rise and fled to America after going to medical school. He became an American citizen then enlisted and served in World War II, helping to liberate prisoners from some of the most horrific concentration camps.

After the war, Dr. Jacobi was on his way to live in Oneonta when the train made a stop in Norwich. "The streets were so crowded with people," his daughter, Nancy, told me, "that it reminded him of New York City, and he immediately fell in love with the little town." He never made it to Oneonta, as those were the glory days of Norwich, when the pharmaceutical business was booming. Pepto-Bismol and Chloraseptic were both invented there, in fact.

He set up his practice and went on to deliver over 8,500 babies. No wonder I regularly ran into someone he'd brought into the world.

Every time I ran into his daughter around town, we hugged. "I love the house," I would tell her.

"I love that you're in the house. The other night, I was driving down the highway and I looked up on the hill—it did my heart good to see the lights on," she said, adding that we turned the lights on in more ways than one.

That made me smile.

We lived in that wonderful house for two years, and when we moved someone else moved in. But to me, it will always be known as the Jacobi House.

Thank you, Dr. Jacobi. It has been an honor to be part of your history.

FINDING THE GOOD IN GOODBYE

And when he had said these things, he knelt down and prayed with them all. Then they all wept freely, and fell on Paul's neck and kissed him, sorrowing most of all for the words which he spoke, that they would see his face no more. And they accompanied him to the ship.

ACTS 20: 36-38

As the walls of the wonderful Jacobi House became bare and the last of the boxes were packed, I was pleasantly surprised to find that goodbyes didn't weaken our relationships. On the contrary, goodbyes strengthened them.

One friend, for instance, made the more than five hour drive from Vermont to tell us goodbye *and* so she could read to Silas and Dorothy "one more time." Little stinker Silas wouldn't let her, but she forgave him.

"Your friendship means a lot to me," several teary-eyed friends told us during our last week.

"I will miss seeing the Sims family sitting out there every week," our pastor said from the pulpit.

It works both ways as I have expressed the same sentiments. When you have to say goodbye, I've discovered, things that might go otherwise unsaid are freely spoken.

Goodbyes have other advantages as well. Mary, then a rising eighth grader, got a bonus from that goodbye as she was allowed an early Facebook page—a privilege usually reserved for high school at our house.

Of course, there is all that cleaning out that is forced upon you when it is time to say goodbye. "Photo albums are hard to pack," Bethany said. She kept sitting down and looking at them.

"I didn't really want to move," Ben recalled, "but we had moved enough for me to know that we're

187

like arrows and we would go where God aimed us." I remember being pleasantly surprised at what came out of my fifteen year old son's mouth.

Silas was four at the time and kept reviewing the plan with me as he witnessed the packing.

"Someone else will live in this house?"

Yes.

"And we will go to another house?"

Yes.

"Am I going, too?"

Of course, I said, amazed at such a question.

We said goodbye to Matthew, as he reported to West Point before we left, but we had a send-off for him. Bonfire, ultimate frisbee, dishes of food, and dozens of people. The goodbye, I think, reaffirmed the friendships he'd made during his short time in Norwich.

"What can I do for you before you leave?" droves of friends asked, offering meals or cleaning or both. I gratefully accepted any and all help at that point, since my growing belly prohibited bending and I was too tired to cook for my small army.

Goodbyes aren't all bad, I've concluded. If you look hard enough, you can find the good in goodbye every time.

NO OFFENSE, BUT— ✴

And this I pray, that your love may abound still more and more in
knowledge and all discernment, that you may approve the things
that are excellent, that you may be sincere and without offense
till the day of Christ, being filled with the fruits of righteousness
which are by Jesus Christ, to the glory and praise of God.

PHILIPPIANS 1:9-11

One afternoon my eighth grader, Mary, came home and told me her lab partner turned to her during class and said, "No offense, but I really don't want to work with you."

The next day, seven year old Dorothy got off the school bus and shared that after hearing her rendition of "Tomorrow" from *Little Orphan Annie*, her classmate said to her, "No offense, but that sounded horrible."

Perhaps it has its place, but saying "no offense" before a statement does not give a friend license to drop a verbal bomb.

What's next? No offense, but:
You're ugly.
You're an idiot.

I am superior to you in every way.

Once I was telling a friend what a pistol my then four year old Silas was. After describing several of his antics and my responses to them, she simply said, "He is the baby," then quickly added, "No offense."

"None taken," I said, as I knew she was just trying to help me see Silas from a different perspective, telling me as a friend. Being the baby of eight myself, I got it.

It all comes down to teaching kids manners; reinforcing plain, old-fashioned common courtesy. Instruct kids on what is appropriate to say to someone, and urge them to check their motives for saying it. Remind them that because people have feelings, it is not acceptable to say everything and anything that pops into their heads—no matter how much better it might make them feel.

No offense, but if we don't remind them, who will?

Margie Sims

WHAT WE LIKE ✦ ABOUT FLORIDA

A friend loves at all times, and a brother is born for adversity.
PROVERBS 17:17

I took the chicken out to thaw. And the ribs. I cooked everything in the freezer, and then took down the pictures and began packing up the house. The Sims family was headed to Virginia.

Spending a year in south Florida was like having a long beach vacation. Imagine after almost a decade in the northeast, having thirteen months without winter! Here's a fact for you: South Florida's winter is warmer than Vermont's spring. I dressed Hope in only a sleeper in January, but years earlier had to bundle Dorothy up when it was May in Vermont. The things you learn from living in different places.

New opportunity awaited us in Virginia, but before we made our exit, I tweaked the Sims' family

birthday tradition a bit. Instead of "What I Like About You," we did "What I Like About Florida."

The Captain said the beach was his favorite thing. He liked it best when the kids and I came along, but he often went alone for a solitary sunrise. Ever the romantic, he always found a "shell of the day" for me. In Vermont it was "leaf of the day," and New York was "wildflower of the day." Husbands, watch and learn.

When I asked Mom Dot for her favorite thing about Florida, she said, "The road that leads out of here." No offense, Floridians, she didn't like the heat. "Florida has the most beautiful sky of anywhere I have ever seen," she added. I agreed. There is something intriguing about

191

those clouds scattered across the wide sky.

Mary said she learned so much about herself and life—eighth grade was a hard year to move. She wouldn't brag on herself, but we discovered she was a beast (to borrow a term from Ben) in the pool—third fastest girl on the swim team, and only a freshman at the time. "She needs to be swimming," her coach said to me when I stopped to thank her for helping Mary find her niche. Her dad had already found a team in Virginia.

Emma is my nature girl (and one of the best cooks I know, but that's a topic for another day). She liked the "crazy animals and plants." With grasshoppers the size of small birds, leapin' lizards that darted across your path, and birds as tall as her brother Silas, it was a nature lover's paradise. Emma has the pictures to prove it.

Ben said he liked the people. Since Ben was about to attend his third high school in three years, I was glad Ben liked people—and people liked Ben. He will do well anywhere you move, folks often said. I agreed, but I knew I had to be careful not to leave him on auto-pilot. I would add to anyone who has one or more low-maintenance kids, be sure and keep your finger on their emotional pulse. Never stop paying attention.

As for me, I say the same thing I say every time we move: the friends I've made. It didn't happen right away, but as our year in Florida unfolded, I made friendships as deep as the Atlantic. The folks that surprised us with everything from dinner to donuts, and then helped us pack and clean on loading day, that had Silas over to play when he seemed a little lost watching the furniture go onto the truck. Friends hugged my neck at church Sunday morning and rang my doorbell all that weekend to tell us how much they would miss our family. Mom Dot says I have a gift for friendship, but I tell her I am needy that way.

As soon as Hurricane Isaac simmered down, our caravan once again hit the road. While I couldn't take the beach or the south Florida sky with me, I knew I would take along the friends I'd made.

That's what *I* like about Florida.

DIVIN' IN

*For I know the thoughts that I think toward you," says the
Lord, "thoughts of peace and not of evil, to give you a future
and a hope. Then you will call upon Me and go and pray to
Me, and I will listen to you. And you will seek Me and find
Me, when you search for Me with all your heart.*

JEREMIAH 29:11-13

The summer the Sims family pulled into Virginia, we didn't know a soul. But three weeks after we arrived, we had visited three churches and attended Ben's varsity football game. Next up was Emma's first cross country meet, but not before fifteen year old Mary made a speech at school to convince her classmates why she should be their vice-president.

To put it simply, we dove right in.

Captain Fun and I have lived in five states since the day we said "I do," and I'm convinced that whether you move once or a dozen times, diving in is the only way to survive a move. That's why when the nice folks from the Presbyterian church called and invited me to their "Mov-

ing On After Moving In" small group, I told 'em to count me in—and oldest daughter, Bethany, too. It's why I found a MOPS (Mothers of Preschoolers) group right away, as well as a mid-week ladies' Bible study, which Bethany also attended with me. Small group groupies, we often joked on the way home.

Yes, I had boxes (but don't I always have boxes?). Yes, it was getting "a little nippy" outside as my dad used to say, and I wasn't positive we all owned coats after living in south Florida. But boxes and coats could wait—a little while, anyway. I learned what I needed for myself and my family to feel connected in a new place, and that is relationships.

I must pause to say that the people of Virginia were accommodating. From the grocery store to the playground, folks were friendly. The bus stop was my favorite—with a dozen kids and half a dozen moms, it was like a little mom pep rally twice a day. Being the people person that I am, I tried not to come on too strong. I had been gone from my familiar Florida friends for three weeks, after all, and my talk tank was low.

We were quite fond of Florida by the time we left, and we wouldn't forget the friends we made there.

What a privilege it had bee to live eight miles from the beach for a year; to have baby Hope in December during the mild winter. Oh, how it blessed me to walk into First Baptist Church of Stuart on that first Sunday in Florida only to discover I knew the pastor's family well thanks to our Memphis roots.

Hindsight showed me that God navigated our move to Florida. Consequently, I quickly fell in love with Virginia and anticipated watching His plan unfold.

EVERYBODY? NOT ✴ ON MY WATCH

Beloved, I beg you as sojourners and pilgrims, abstain from fleshly lusts which war against the soul, having your conduct honorable among the Gentiles, that when they speak against you as evildoers, they may, by your good works which they observe, glorify God in the day of visitation.

1 PETER 2:11-12

I wanted to ride my bike to the mall with my BFF when I was about twelve. My mother said no.

I told her *everybody* rode their bikes to the mall.

"If everybody jumped off a cliff, would you jump, too?" she asked.

Why do all my friends' mothers say that? I thought.

When I was seventeen, a guy who was well over twenty-one asked me on a date. My mother said I had to wait until I was eighteen to go out with him. So I did.

In college, a foreign student invited me to his apartment. "I will cook dinner for you," he said in his thick, mysterious accent.

"I can guarantee you he has more in mind than dinner," my mother said.

Conversations between kids and parents have changed, it seems. Nowadays they go something like this:

"Why wait until I am twenty-one to drink? Everybody drinks before they are twenty-one."

"Fine, then," say Mom and Dad. "We will host the party so we can supervise and make sure no one drives home under the influence."

At the last high school my kids attended, a banner hung on the gate from prom to graduation proclaiming "Parents Who Host Lose the Most." Really? We have to have a giant sign to encourage us not to host underage drinking?

When one daughter was in the spring musical during her senior year, I volunteered our house for the cast party.

"Well, Mom," she said, "I already mentioned it, and they want to have a coed sleepover. I told them my parents would never go for that."

"How about the girls sleep over and the boys leave at midnight?"

"I offered that, too, but they said they would find a house where the parents either didn't care or weren't paying attention."

What happened to the jumping off the cliff analogy? What happened to *That's not healthy, That's not right, You're too young* or *It's illegal.*

"Why try and stop them when they are just going to do it anyway?" I hear repeatedly.

Because they need to know it's wrong when they do it. How will they know if we parents don't tell them?

Wrong: the opposite of right. Introduce your kids to the word.

Most kids want boundaries. All kids need guidance. They all need to know parents care enough to say *no*.

It is no wonder kids are convinced everybody's doing everything. Instead of encouraging the common sense it takes to not tumble over the cliff with the crowd, parents are packing kids a parachute to protect them from consequences, then acting as private escort right up to the edge.

Say no, offer guidance, be the bad guy (it's in the job description). Will kids always make the right choices? Maybe not. But they will know the difference between right and wrong, and they won't have to wonder if you care.

THE MEANING OF A MEAL ✦

When the day began to wear away, the twelve came and said to Him, 'Send the multitude away, that they may go into the surrounding towns and country, and lodge and get provisions; for we are in a deserted place here.' But He said to them, 'You give them something to eat.' And they said, 'We have no more than five loaves and two fish, unless we go and buy food for all these people.' For there were about five thousand men.

LUKE 9:12-14

I love to feed people. It is odd, because cooking really isn't my favorite thing. I suspect, though, that I enjoy taking meals to people because of all the meals that have been brought to me. Ridiculous amounts of food have been delivered upon the birth of each baby, for sure. And I will never forget after the loss of my mom how our Sunday school class, to which we were still fairly new, fed us for weeks.

There is something about taking a meal to a new mom, a sick friend, or showing up with a "breakfast basket" for someone who is down. It blesses people. It blesses me.

I remember when I took a meal to a friend after her surgery. I had to *tell* her I was bringing it. If I asked if I *could* bring it, she would have brushed me off with an, "Oh, no, that's all right." So, I told her that we (her other friends and I) had a secret meeting behind her back and we were providing dinner for a week or so. Period. She laughed. She knew she was cornered.

Illnesses, funerals, blue days, birthdays—food makes people *feel* better. If you know someone who is ill or down and you have thought about taking them some food, do it. Easy or elaborate, a meal hits the mark every time.

 BOO!

Do not withhold good from those to whom it is due,
when it is in the power of your hand to do so. Do
not say to your neighbor, 'Go and come back, and
tomorrow I will give it.' When you have it with you.

PROVERBS 3:27-28

Even if you don't celebrate Halloween, booing is a great way to reach out in friendship to neighbors you don't know. Besides, with scary stuff daily in the headlines, it might be the thing to ease your kids' minds. Whenever we move into a new neighborhood, in fact, I always consider starting it myself.

I will never forget the first time we were booed shortly after we moved to Virginia, proving once again that, yes, Virginia really is for lovers. It was a Saturday night, after dark, and the Sims family was sitting in the den enjoying the fireplace and a little TV when the doorbell rang. The kids ran to answer, but no one was there—only a bucket of goodies and a note that read "You've just been booed!"

I don't get the warm fuzzies very often, but this made me fuzzy all over. It was a feel good moment for the whole family. "What kind of neighborhood have we moved into that has such fun traditions?" said Captain Fun. This one had his name all over it.

The older kids tried to figure out who booed us while the younger kids squealed as they tore into candy, small games, and neon vampire teeth. The first ever, I must say, that they could call their own since we don't typically encourage imitating vampires at our house.

The following Monday, when I consulted the Moms at the Bus Stop (I gave my new friends an official title since they frequently find their way into my writing), they confirmed it and gave me some booing guidance. I reiterated how over-the-top friendly I was finding Virginia. I hope they aren't tired of hearing it because I will probably tell them again.

When the kids got home from school, we went to the dollar store to collect the loot for two booings. That night, after dark, we delivered. I think I was more excited about it than the kids. It takes a lot to make that happen.

If you decide to start the booing tradition in your neighborhood, here are a few guidelines:

- Boo two families in one night by ringing the doorbell after dark and leaving the boo bucket on the porch. Try to get away before the door is answered so you can stay anonymous.

- Try to know something about the families you boo. One of my first targets, for instance, had an empty nest so I included a copy of my favorite novel for her. (Jan Karon's Mitford series.)

- Finally, keep it easy. "No pressure!" the note in the boo bucket said. Good thing, since technically I was supposed to boo within 48 hours of being booed. Uh, it took me a few hours longer than that. That's okay—the note gave me permission. I kept it fun.

It's a scary thought, but I might have had more fun than Captain Fun himself.

✦ THE MOMS AT THE BUS STOP

Now all who believed were together, and had all things in common and sold their possessions and goods, and divided them among all, as anyone had need. So, continuing daily with one accord in the temple, and breaking bread from house to house, they ate their food with gladness and simplicity of heart, praising God and having favor with all the people.

ACTS 2:44-47a

Captain Fun and I have moved many times since we got married in 1986. I have said it before: I don't mind moving. I like seeing new places and meeting new people. The diversity of the different regions of the country intrigues me.

Sometimes, unlike myself, the women are reserved. It takes me a while to convince them to be my friend, but I usually find a way. I am needy like that. Once in a while, though, I meet such a friendly group of women, I know I will never forget them. Meet The Moms at the Bus Stop.

Rarely have I had a warmer welcome than The Moms at the Bus Stop offered me when we arrived in Virginia. From our first introduc-tion, those moms were as warm as a southern spring day.

About fifteen kids and six moms gathered every morning. From our first introduction, they took me in. Sometimes, especially when I was in my "I'm new here and I need a friend" mode, I was sure I came on too strong. First of all, I talked too much. I usually had half a doz-en kids with me at any given time. Then add to that the fact that I could have easily passed for Hope's grandmother... Well, sometimes, folks don't quite get me.

But The Moms at the Bus Stop were unfazed. "Welcome to Vir-ginia!" I heard repeatedly on the first day of school. They told me to put their cell phone numbers in my contacts, then begged me to call them for any other help I might need. During the weeks following, they showed up at my door with food, hand me downs, and all sorts of information "just in case."

The Moms at the Bus Stop were generous, and I gladly received car seats, baby bouncers, clothes and even a stroller. Whether I need a pediatrician, a soccer team, or the best consignment shop, the Moms at the Bus Stop pointed me in the right direction. "Everything I ever needed to know, I learned at the bus stop," a friend of mine joked recently.

The Moms at the Bus Stop also embraced motherhood in a way that was refreshing. They were room mothers, troop leaders and carpool drivers. One morning near the end of the year, they informed me that on the last day of school, the plan was to greet the kids with Popsicles and silly string as they got off the bus. Then it was off to a neighborhood pool party. Why was I not surprised?

But my favorite thing about them was that they were never in a hurry. Once the bus pulled away (and they all stayed until it did), it was not uncommon for us to chat for another twenty minutes. Always about the kids, of course.

In all my years of raising kids, I have often been isolated in my role as a mom. It felt so good to have company, community, camaraderie with these very warm women.

By the next school year, I was standing at another bus stop, as our family purchased a nearby home the following summer. I had to tell them, explain to them, express to them how I felt. "Thank you, Moms at the Bus Stop. I will miss your smiling faces every morning and afternoon. If every group of women were as friendly as you, every mom would find all the support she craves in this complicated job of motherhood," I proclaimed, adding a disclaimer.

Don't be surprised if I still show up at 9:00 AM once in a while. I'm needy that way, you know.

SECTION FIVE:
FUN

Fun is a vital ingredient to family life, so these stories are just for fun and a little light on the spiritual side. While the Captain finds the fun in every opportunity, I let the fun come to me. We make a good team.

A MOTHER'S NEW YEAR'S RESOLUTION

But let patience have its perfect work, that you
may be perfect and complete, lacking nothing.

JAMES 1:4

I will remember that a bad day is a good day when no one's throwing up.

I will be more concerned about the child than the carpet when she is throwing up.

I will, without apology, be the nutrition, television, and hygiene police.

I will use the television as a babysitter—on rare occasion and as if it cost $10 an hour.

I won't accept criticism from parents who have half the kids and twice the money.

More kids and less house is more fun than more house and fewer kids.

More house and more kids is more fun than either of the above.

Cleanliness is not next to godliness.

I will cheerfully accept muddy glasses of water and jelly smeared kisses.

I will always deliver on a promise—be it for reward or punishment.

I will lower my voice instead of raising it when correcting my children.

I will convince myself that a camping trip is a vacation.

I will convince myself that a grocery store trip is not a vacation.

I will remember that teenagers and two-year-olds sometimes have a lot in common.

Disrespect in the form of back talk, grunts, or the rolling of even half an eyeball will not be tolerated in my home.

I'm the mother, I'm the mother, I'm the mother.

I will not allow any amount of begging, pleading, or whining to prevent me from teaching my children to work hard.

I will pretend not to be shocked when my teenager confides in me.

I will set a "Do what I do, not just what I say" example for my children.

No matter what, I will treat my children like the treasures that they are.

I will not merely parent on the side, I will parent with abandon.

CAPTAIN FUN STRIKES AGAIN ✳

*As iron sharpens iron, so a man sharpens
the countenance of his friend.*

PROVERBS 27:17

Writer John Trent says people basically have one of four personalities: beaver, lion, otter, or retriever. My husband, aka Captain Fun, is a fun-loving otter who is always trying to force fun on me. It gets annoying when you're a working beaver.

When we took our daughter Bethany to New York City for the day for her twenty-first birthday, Captain Fun had to bring the whole family back forty-eight hours later. No problem. It was only eight kids and Grandma.

When the temperature is less than fifty degrees, he'll ask who wants to go for a walk. When it's above fifty degrees, he wants to play baseball. Or soccer. Or football.

During TV shows, he rewinds funny commercials.

When we go to the lake, he begs me to swim. I prefer the lawn chair, thank you.

And one winter when the snow measured almost two feet on our hill, sledding was the order of the day. I was doing my usual beaver-like activities—sweeping, cooking, laundry. After all, I had been gone for five days and things were a little messy.

"Can I talk you into sledding?" he said, poking his frosty face around the door.

"No. It's Sunday. I'm resting."

"Aw, come on. Your children need to have one memory of you sledding with them."

"They do," I said. "I have pictures."

"No, that was the older kids—the grown ones. The younger kids don't have any memories of you sledding with them."

Darn. He was right. But winter is far from over in upstate New York, I argued. Captain Fun was not going to get to me this time.

I swept for a few more minutes, stomping around, listing out loud all the reasons why I didn't want to go out. Then I went out.

"You're out!" he exclaimed. Surprise, surprise.

We rode double down the driveway, and I laughed hysterically on each trip. Three year old Silas went repeatedly all by himself. The fast-er he went, the louder he squealed. The teens and preteens came out when they heard Mom was sledding. (Better come, Captain Fun told them, it's the only chance you'll get to sled with Mom in your childhood.)

After the sledding, he insisted on a snowball fight. I tolerated it. (Hitting him with snowballs helped.)

I hate to admit it, but if it weren't for him, I would never take the time to have fun with the family.

"Thanks for coming out," he said.

No, thank you, Captain Fun, for helping this beaver remember to look a little more like an otter.

THE OTHER SIDE OF ME ✸

For though I am free from all men, I have made myself a servant to all, that I might win the more; and to the Jews I became as a Jew, that I might win Jews; to those who are under the law, as under the law, that I might win those who are under the law; to those who are without law, as without law (not being without law toward God, but under law toward Christ), that I might win those who are without law; to the weak I became as weak, that I might win the weak. I have become all things to all men, that I might by all means save some.

I CORINTHIANS 9:19-22

I discovered another side of myself. It was sort of by accident, but it brought me closer to where my kids live.

It happened suddenly one afternoon many years ago, as my children were climbing into our mammoth white, fifteen passenger van, a vehicle my teenagers fondly referred to as Moby Dick. It struck me as comical that all these kids climbing into the van were mine. I suddenly felt like a bus driver. "Move to the back of the bus," I commanded in a nasally voice which brought Edith Bunker, of *All in the Family* fame, to mind.

Mary and Emma, then four and five, squealed with delight, "Who are you?" they asked. Again, my mind returned to my 70's TV childhood, and Arnold Horshack from *Welcome Back Kotter* was the first person who popped into mind. "I'm Mrs. Horshack, a friend of your muth-uhs," I replied. I then proceeded to give them nicknames, reserved for use only by their new friend. For the rest of that school year, Mrs. Horshack put the younger kids on the bus most mornings. "Good-byyyye Elvis, Tina, Annie," she called out to the children who in "real life" were Ben, Mary, and Emma.

"Catch my kisses, Mrs. Horshack!" they yelled from the end of the driveway, wildly waving their arms. "One for you and one for Mommy."

Over the years, Mrs. Horshack has frequently shown up at family occasions or milestones. When baby number eight was on the way, for instance, Mrs. Horshack broke the news. "I know a secret about your muth-uhhh," she announced one evening at dinner. Though their eyes widened upon hearing the news, it wasn't until I, the real mom, confirmed it that they actually believed me.

In truth, I'm like any other mom. I get stressed, I lose my temper. I sometimes even yell at my kids. I'm often in a hurry and don't always listen to what they have to say. As I've mentioned before, playing is hard work for me. But these are not the traits I want my kids to remember when they reminisce about their childhood. Enter Mrs. Horshack.

While the average mom might excel at running her house, Mrs. Horshack is a pro at having fun. She chases kids around with the vacuum cleaner, playfully reminds them to use their manners at the table, makes spontaneous pit stops for doughnuts, and always, always makes them laugh. As the real mom, I have a bad habit of telling my children I'll play with them "in a minute," but somehow pretending to be this ebullient lady equips me. Mrs. Horshack makes it happen.

Some of my kids had less affection for my alter ego. Teenagers at the time, Tiger (a.k.a. Stanley) and Bethany (a.k.a. Eunice), as well as my then-middle schooler, Matthew (Melvin), used to roll their eyes and beg me not to embarrass them in front of their friends. I wouldn't do that, I reassured them, and neither would Mrs. Horshack, thank you very much.

Sometimes Mrs. Horshack doesn't show up for long stretches of time. The summer our family relocated from Memphis to Vermont (and our youngest was just six weeks old), it took her months to catch up with us. I was simply too tired to be silly. But it wasn't until she finally re-appeared that I realized how important it was that I interact with my kids in this way.

"Oh, Mrs. Horshack, I love you! Where have you been?" my then seven year old Mary (alias Tina) said, a bit of pleading in her voice.

Mrs. Horshack reassured her that she had been looking for them, and when she went to their old house, they were all gone. "And when did you move to Vermont, anyway?" she asked. "You have to tell Mrs. Horshack these things." Just like old friends, we picked up right where we'd left off.

Sometimes my younger kids try

to distract me when they have been mischievous or I'm in a foul mood. "Mrs. Horshack?" they'll say, trying to call her to rescue them from real life and their grumpy mom.

"She is most certainly not here," I answer in my sternest voice. Other times, I'll find it in me to be silly only to be accused of being Mrs. Horshack. "No, it's me," I say, reminding them that I was the person who created Mrs. Horshack in the first place.

My alter ego has become such a part of our family that I wonder if sometimes I shouldn't set her a place at the table. After all, who knows how long this tradition will last. I wonder if my kids will outgrow her or if she might evolve into Granny Horshack someday?

It doesn't matter—as long as they remember that their mom went out of her way to introduce them to the other side—the silly side—of me.

THE BOY IN THE CHICKEN SUIT

A merry heart does good, like medicine,
but a broken spirit dries the bones.

PROVERBS 17:22

I have always loved a good bargain. I shop for next year's winter coats at the end of the season. I buy next year's bathing suits at the end of the summer. After Halloween, I like to see what deals I can get on costumes. (When you're a mom of many, you don't ask what everyone wants to be for Halloween. Instead, you spread out all the costumes in the dress up box and say, "Pick one!")

I was proud of the chicken suit I had bought from Kohl's for around $9.00 on clearance. The fabric was not only durable but came complete with separate pull-on chicken legs and a hood! Whichever kid could fit into it always had a lot of fun with it. Cory took it a step further.

He greeted me one morning when he was around seven years old. "Mom, can I wear my chicken suit to school one day?"

"Well, you'll have to ask your teacher," I said, certain she would say no because it would disrupt the class.

He burst through the door later that day. "She said I could wear it!" I had no choice but to keep my word, but I didn't think he would go through with it.

Next morning, he came down for breakfast in his chicken suit. To catch the bus.

"Why is Cory wearing a chicken suit to school?" his siblings asked.

"He feels like it," I said, as if they had asked why the grass was green.

"I am so glad I am not riding the bus today," said my then-high schooler Matthew.

Breakfast was over; it was time to catch the bus. Out marched three kids and one chicken to stand at the end of the driveway on our somewhat busy street. But Cory didn't just stand there. He waved at the passing cars. He flapped his wings. He did the chicken dance.

"I am so glad I am not riding the bus," repeated Matthew.

I doubled over with laughter as I watched the puzzled drivers pass by. My sides ached and tears streamed down my face as the bus pulled up and I saw the reaction of all on board. I was still cracking up as the bus pulled away.

"How did it go?" I asked Cory when he got home, still in his chicken suit.

"Great! The other kids chased me around the playground at recess yelling, 'We want chicken!'"

"I think it is great that you wore a chicken suit to school just because you felt like it, Cory. Your classmates will always remember the day you came to school in a chicken suit."

He said thanks and went on his way. Somehow, I thought, I got a lot more for my $9.00 than just a chicken suit. I also got a memory I will never forget.

✦ THAT SOUTHERN DRAWL

Let your speech always be with grace, seasoned with salt,
that you may know how you ought to answer each one.
COLOSSIANS 4: 6

I grew up in Memphis, Tennessee, but I've been out of the south for over a decade. Even though all but Silas and Hope were born in the south, my younger ones tease me relentlessly about my southern drawl.

"I am going to drive y'all home," I stated on the way to school one day. The statement was innocent, harmless. That's when the attack came, unprovoked. "Dri-ive yawl. What is dri-ive yawl?" asked Cory, my then nine-year-old.

I spoke more slowly—easy for a southerner, but he still didn't understand.

I broke it down for him. "I am going to drive you all. Y'all means you all, as in all of you. I am going to drive all of you home from school."

He got it.

"Mom, why don't you pass that car in front of us?" Mary, thirteen at the time, asked me as we poked along the winding road.

"There's a double yellow line," I said.

Again, an unprovoked attack came from the back seat as cackles filled the car. "A dubble yella li-ine! What is a dubble yella li-ine?"

And then, Dorothy, who was six, mimicked the way I turn one syllable words into two syllable words. I explained to her that, for a southerner, there are no one syllable words. We really can't help it.

"Maybe one day you'll talk normal," she said.

"Someday we might move back to the south, and y'all will be the

214

ones who talk funny," I sometimes warned my children.

Try as I might to keep my speech graceful and salty with my children, unlike a southerner, they never heard past the "y'all."

COUSIN FERNIE

Correct your son and he will give you rest;
yes, he will give delight to your soul.

PROVERBS 29:17

Why is it that ten year old boys resist showers, vegetables, and brushing their teeth?

When he was ten, I realized that whenever I told Cory (of "chicken suit" fame) to do something—anything—that was healthy for him, he ignored me. Or he tried.

"Go take a shower, Cory," I said one night. Not an unusual request from a mother on a Sunday night. He stood there without acknowledging that I had spoken.

"Cory, go take a shower," I said again.

"I don't need a shower. I just took one."

"You did not just take one, and you do need a shower."

He trudged away to gather his pajamas and a towel, reappearing a minute later. "The bathroom smells bad."

"That is the nature of bathrooms. Go take a shower."

"But it really smells bad. Come smell it."

"I don't need to smell it because no matter what it smells like, you are taking a shower."

"But Cousin Fernie died that way!" His final objection before taking a shower.

Meet Cousin Fernie—the family fall guy.

It was my wry mother-in-law who first introduced me to Cousin Fernie. Mom Dot is, by her own admission, a bit of a worrier and tends to "awfulize" at times. When one of the kids had a nosebleed, a stomach ache, or a fever, she was often of the opinion that I needed to call the doctor. Years ago, it seemed Cousin Fernie had that same condition and died from it. Twice.

Cousin Fernie goes way back to Mom Dot's own mother-in-law, she tells me. Whenever one of her own kids had an accident, her mother-in-law would shake her head back and forth very slowly while whispering, "It's the worst death in the world. In fact, it was the end of old Cousin Fernie."

"I said I would never be like my mother-in-law," Mom Dot sometimes warned me, "but here I am turning into her."

With accidents and illnesses being the norm at our house, I confess I have become a bit calloused to them. If there is blood (and lots of it) I might take a trip to the ER, but even then it's not a guarantee. We have had broken bones, stitches, concussions, surgeries, chicken pox, strep throat, ear infections, and the swine flu to name a few. Cousin Fernie had all these conditions— and died from most of them.

"Cory, I only make you do all these things because I love you and I want you to be happy," I chided him one morning when he (gasp!) resisted going to school.

"I think you are trying to torture me," he said.

If torture is defined as a mother making her kids do what's good for them on a regular basis, then so be it.

I have a sneaking suspicion that even Cousin Fernie never died from that.

AUNT AGNES

Not that I speak in regard to need, for I have learned in whatever state I am, to be content: I know how to be abased, and I know how to abound. Everywhere and in all things I have learned both to be full and to be hungry, both to abound and to suffer need. I can do all things through Christ who strengthens me.

PHILIPPIANS 4: 11-13

My mother-in-law, Mom Dot, told me that she was named Dorothy Alice after her aunt, Agnes Alice.

When Aunt Agnes lost her husband, she went to live with her sister. But no matter how her sister tried to please her, the story goes, she was not happy. "Agnes refuses to be content," she told Mom Dot one day many years ago when they saw one another at a family funeral.

Much like Cousin Fernie, Agnes has become an icon in our family. "Agnes refuses to be content" is a family motto of sorts.

We all have our moments, or even seasons, of discontentment. But I strive not to be like Agnes, and I encourage my children to do the same.

When we moved to a small town in upstate New York, for instance, I felt I had to go looking for contentment. Surely it was an hour away, like the mall, the nearest city, and the airport. But I soon discovered if I looked for the negatives during that season of transition, I would find them. Ditto with the positives. I looked, and I found them.

During the wintertime, the weather made me squirm...or freeze. One day, for instance, our high hovered around thirty degrees. This made me wrestle with discontentment when most of the country was thawing. But, as some of my Facebook friends pointed out, the sun was shining and spring was not far behind. Contentment was attainable—I needed to look up at the blue sky instead of down at the old, cold, dingy snow.

Finding contentment can be the difference between calm and turmoil. It is the mom who says "Get the camera" instead of "Get the mop" when the baby dumps spaghetti on her head.

It is recognizing dirty kids, dirty laundry, and dirty dishes are signs of blessing.

Contentment is a powerful thing, a choice, a gift. I have discovered in the everyday routine of life, it can be found if you look for it. However, if we're not careful, motherhood can constantly compel us toward discontentment.

Be it winter weather, constant cleanup, or even another move on the horizon, I will choose contentment by looking for the sun, grabbing the camera, unpacking the bags, the kids, and the pets. Then, unlike Aunt Agnes, I will not refuse to be content. Consequently, no matter how many moves we make or where we land, I know I'll find it every time.

✦ DOZENS OF COUSINS

God sets the solitary in families; He brings out those who are bound into prosperity. But the rebellious dwell in a dry land.

PSALM 68:6

When I was a kid, we went to Little Rock every Memorial Day to see my Dad's family. He was the oldest of eight kids with six sisters and a brother.

"Mom, which aunt is that?" I would whisper to my mother when no one was looking. She always told me who was who, but no matter how many years we returned, I never got my aunts straight until I was grown.

With sixteen first cousins and nine second cousins, my younger kids had the same problem with remembering who's who in the family. Living 1,300 miles away didn't help.

I started a "Family Bulletin Board" and hung it in the hallway off the kitchen. Anytime we got a new picture of the cousins, it went on the board. Every so often I'd see one of my kids studying the pictures, trying to put faces with names.

"Is that Uncle Rusty?" my daughter Mary inquired, pointing at one of the pictures.

"Well, that is Rusty," I laughed, "but he isn't your uncle, he's your cousin. He is the son of my oldest sister, your Aunt Debbie. In fact," I continued, unaware that Mary's eyes had glazed over with Too Much Information, "he is the oldest of all the cousins. I was only eight years old when he was born."

That bit of history brought her back to the moment. "You became an aunt when you were *eight*?"

"Yes. Then your cousin, Brian,

was born just two weeks later."

"He has the twins?" Emma chimed in.

"That's right!" I exclaimed, delighted over a correct answer.

Their confusion was understandable, considering the distance between us. But one day, family confusion attained a new level. My daughter-in-law's mother came over for a visit.

"Dorothy," she said to my six-year-old, "I have pictures of Tiger kayaking down in Florida with Becky."

Dorothy looked confused. "Tiger was kayaking?"

"Tiger, your brother," said Heather. "You know, you were in their wedding last summer?"

"Oh, oh!" said Dorothy. "I thought you were talking about Tiger, our cat."

Dorothy saw Tiger, the cat, a lot more often than she saw Tiger, her brother, seventeen years her senior, so I guess that was understandable.

A few days later, I was talking about cousin Lu from the other side of the family and how her birthday was coming up.

"I thought cousin Lu had died," Cory said. "Isn't she the same as Cousin Fernie?"

This was serious. "No, no, no." I laughed. "Cousin Lu is alive and well. Cousin Fernie has died many times of many ailments. Fernie isn't real, Lu is, and her birthday is coming up." We all had a good laugh, as we always do over family confusion.

But at least one thing is always clear: A whole lotta family means a whole lotta love. There is no confusion about that.

✦ THE GREEN TENNIS BALL

*And whoever gives one of these little ones only a cup
of cold water in the name of a disciple, assuredly, I
say to you, he shall by no means lose his reward.*

MATTHEW 10:42

We celebrated Matthew's nineteenth birthday shortly before he left for West Point. I wasn't sure how many birthdays we would have him at home while he was in school. Consequently, our Sims birthday tradition, "What I Like About You" was especially meaningful. Until he mentioned the green tennis ball.

"What is the green tennis ball?" his friend inquired.

He had to ask, didn't he?

Matthew cleared his throat as if he were choking back tears. "Uh, when I was in kindergarten, we were learning our colors, and the color of the week was green."

"And tennis balls are green," I interjected.

He shot me a look. "I told Mom I needed to take something green to school."

"He told me as we were walking out the door."

"She grabbed a tennis ball. I said, 'That's not green, that's yellow,' and she said, 'It's green. It's lime green.'" Another pause. "We sat down for circle time, and one kid had a dollar, another kid brought in a leaf. Then my turn came, and I…I held up my tennis ball. 'That's not green,' the teacher said. Gasps could be heard all over the room as every eye turned and looked at me."

"And he was scarred for life," I said. Even though we Googled it, and the answer came up that tennis balls were yellowish green. In fact, it seems there is an ongoing debate about the color of tennis balls. There. That proves it. I'm innocent.

"I have forgiven you for the green tennis ball incident," Matthew said, wiping his eyes.

"Thank you," I said. It is a conversation we have at least once a year.

Honestly, I hate the thought of my little five-year-old Matthew sinking into his seat as the teacher proclaimed, "That's not green." I am certain that in his young mind every classmate did glare at him as if he had committed an unpardonable deed.

But I am afraid my kids' stories don't stop with the green tennis ball. There's the time I left Ben at church, the time I left Cory at home, and the time I showed up at the wrong field with the wrong kid on the wrong night, to name a few. But all these years later, they still give us something to laugh over. Sometimes it is my mistakes, sometimes theirs.

But always, always with the understanding that families love each other—warts, tennis balls, and all.

 HELLO, SUMMER

*She watches over the ways of her household
and does not eat the bread of idleness.*

PROVERBS 31:27

"You know you will have the kids at home all day, every day pretty soon?" Mom Dot, always the eternal optimist, said to me once when school was drawing to a close.

I responded with the truth. I love summer. I love everything about it. Scheduled activities slow to a crawl with Sunday morning church practically the only commitment on the calendar. Longer days meant later afternoons at the beach, which begged for quick, easy dinners. Late nights meant later mornings. (The kids, that is—I am always up early for some solitude. As the saying goes, you snooze, you lose.) Top it off with a week of Vacation Bible School and a family vacation, and you have a perfectly satisfying summer season.

I used to wing summer, but now I do have some summer strategies. I think it was the day that one of my teenagers came down the stairs in a green bathrobe at 11:00 A.M. and, with furrowed brow, asked, "What's for lunch?"

Uh, for some reason, a light bulb came on. I knew immediately I needed more structure.

Chore lists were posted ("I remember the Chore List!" Bethany chimed in when she called as I was printing it.) Among other things, each kid oversaw one room of the house. Six able-bodied kids at home in charge of six rooms practically covered the whole house.

I regularly perused the 75% off

shelf at my favorite consignment store. I was there before school got out, in fact, and the owner commented on my large purchase of games, books and puzzles. "I have several kids at home and summer is here," I said.

"Say no more," she replied. (And after my credit, my total was only $16.00, to boot.)

If summer turns you into an uptight mama, take heart. With a little effort, even the most disorganized moms, like myself, can embrace every part of summer—including when it's over.

 HAPPY NOISES

*He who blesses his friend with a loud voice, rising
early in the morning, it will be counted a curse to him.*

PROVERBS 27:14

My house was noisy. A bunch of kids, three adults, two cats and a dog.

Mornings were brimming with activity; dinnertime was bustling with chatter. In case you hadn't noticed, I am married to Captain Fun, so evenings were especially loud.

That is why I learned to separate the happy from the unhappy noise.

A whiny child is unhappy noise, as is an escalating argument among siblings.

Squeals of laughter from the den—happy noise. Captain Fun calling out the rules to a game. Ditto.

Silas hitting the piano keys—happy. Silas hitting his sister—unhappy.

You get the idea.

I am a writer. Writing requires solitude, quiet, tranquility.

In the past I would wait for these elusive elements to come to me before I could write. However, the more kids I had, the less they appeared. Consequently, I have learned to write through the racket. While the happy noise is easier to embrace, the unhappy is simply part of it.

When my kids began to launch from the nest, I knew that gradually, yet quickly, both kinds of clamor would fade, and nothing would remain except peace and quiet.

Chances were Captain Fun and I would not be too happy about that.

WHY YOU NEED A VACATION ✳

*Come to Me, all you who labor and are heavy laden, and I
will give you rest. Take My yoke upon you and learn from Me,
for I am gentle and lowly in heart, and you will find rest for
your souls. For My yoke is easy and My burden is light.*

MATTHEW 11:28-30

We were nearing the last day of the Sims' summer vacation. It had been nice and long. And necessary.

Early in our marriage, we couldn't afford a vacation. Or so I thought. Then Captain Fun came to me and declared, "I bet we can go to the beach for $350.00."

"No way," I said. But if anyone could pull off a vacation for four for $350.00, it was Captain Fun. Even back then, he was a pro at having fun.

We stocked the ice chest with sandwich fixings and fried chicken, brought cereal and milk along for breakfast, and filled the remainder of the meals in with cheap fast food—except for that one nice dinner out for fresh seafood, of course. We stayed at Motel 6 in Pensacola, Florida—a reasonable drive from Memphis (our home at the time). Of course, gas was a lot cheaper than it is now.

That was many years and many kids ago. Over the years, every time I thought we coudn't afford a vacation, Captain Fun reminded me of that first time I uttered those words. He still takes it as a challenge.

We have stayed everywhere from two-star to four-star hotels. I prefer the four-star, of course, but we have even resorted to camping when necessary. I still pack sandwiches, we eat a lot of pizza (a cheap way to feed so many), and once we drove through McDonald's and ordered from their dollar menu—11 Mc-

Doubles, 2 McChickens, 11 small fries. We spent less than $25.00. (We had our drinks in the ice chest.) It always freaked out the kid on the other end of the speaker when we showed up, but they survived it.

Best of all, we were all together—something that was becoming more challenging with every passing year. Our first day at our most recent beach vacation, in fact, I was counting noses (like all mothers do) and was delightfully surprised when I counted the last one. All of my kids, I thought, right there in the ocean. Together. My heart filled with gratitude.

So, get out the ice chest. Check out the discount hotels websites. Or pull out the sleeping bags. Whatever it takes, go on those family vacations before your kids are up and out.

Tell them Captain Fun sent you.

SUNDAY MORNING WORKOUT ✦

*And let us consider one another in order to stir up love
and good works, not forsaking the assembling of ourselves
together, as is the manner of some, but exhorting one another,
and so much the more as you see the Day approaching.*

HEBREWS 10:24-25

When down to six kids left at home, going to church on Sunday mornings still often resembled a workout. They often looked much the same, with the occasional variation.

As soon as we found our row of seats, the jockeying for position began. "I put my bulletin on the arm of this chair," Mary, thirteen, would say, "because it is my turn to sit by you." (I admit I did love that my teenage daughter wanted to sit by me.)

As the music began, Silas let out a squeal. Last time he said a hearty, "Amen!" after the morning prayer, so the squeal was an improvement. The rest was a Sunday morning ritual, as predictable as our KFC Sunday lunch.

As we stood to sing, Silas reached for me. "Hold me," he said. I picked him up, his legs dangling down my sides. When the lyrics appeared on the screen, Dorothy came to stand in front of me, taking my free hand and holding it to her cheek. Though the hymn we sang tells us to "lift up holy hands" my hands were occupied most Sundays.

One Sunday, Dorothy was inspired and guided my hand to help her balance as she glided into second position. I quietly chided her, knowing our family is enough of a distraction already.

The special music started. I was getting over a cold, and the tickle in my throat was persistent. I felt a coughing spell coming and tried to find the Tic Tacs in my purse. But every mother knows it is impossible to quietly get a Tic Tac during church. (Why don't they make a rattle proof container?) First Dorothy heard it and in a loud breathy whisper asked, "Can I have a Tic Tac?" *Rattle, rattle, rattle.* This made Silas aware of the opportunity, so of course he also asked for a Tic Tac. More rattling, which notified the rest of the row, and all my kids' hands extended out.

After we were seated for the offering, I crossed my legs and my foot got caught in the chair in front of me, which happened to be the chair of Silas's three-year-old comrade. She pushed her seat cushion with all her muscle, trying to force it down, unaware of what was stopping her. Finally, I freed my foot, certain she and Silas conspired before church.

Dorothy whispered, once again in her loud breathy whisper, that she needed to use the restroom. I sent Mary with her. Silas liked that idea and said he needed to go, too. Captain Fun volunteered to take him.

They returned in time for the last song, and Silas again asked to be held, so I obliged him. This time, though, he pressed his cheek firmly against mine, giving me fish lips as I sang, which delighted him.

As the song concluded, the childcare coordinator asked me if I would be willing to fill in if the volunteer who was scheduled didn't arrive in time for Children's Church. "Of course," I said. It would be a vacation.

She arrived after all, so I sent Dorothy and Silas to Children's Church after the last song and settled in for the sermon from the book of Luke.

My pastor quoted Luke 11:13. "If you then, being evil, know how to give good gifts to your children, how much more will your heavenly Father give the Holy Spirit to those who ask him?"

I am a flawed human, yet I long to give my children every good thing I can, be it Tic Tacs during the special music or fish lips during a song. How much more does my flawless, perfect Heavenly Father long to give to me?

That revelation was well worth the Sunday morning workout.

THE MONDAY MORNING CLUB

And He said to them, 'Come aside by yourselves to a deserted place and rest a while.' For there were many coming and going, and they did not even have time to eat. So they departed to a deserted place in the boat by themselves.

MARK 6:31-32

"I am President of the Monday Morning Club," my mother once told me.

I didn't get it then. Doesn't everyone hate Mondays?

But now I understand—she (herself a mother of eight) relished the back to school season when everybody exited on Monday mornings.

Going through an old journal, I came across this poem I wrote shortly after my mother's death. Don't take it too seriously. I do love summer—sleeping in, swimming all day, sunsets. Sometimes we don't eat dinner until 8:00 in the evening!

After homeschooling for four years, I am well aware that home educators have no such luxury. Ditto for moms who work outside the home. When I found it, though, it made me smile. What's more, the kids got a chuckle out of it, too.

Thanks, Mom, for passing the Presidency down to me. Your sense of humor still inspires me. When school starts, I will do my best to serve the office well.

The Monday Morning Club

There is a club
I am President of.
It isn't to discuss how grand my
garden grows,
Or unearth dark, rich soil to bury
seed I'll sow.
It isn't a club of the literary sect,
(But only because I haven't penned
a masterpiece—yet.)
This club is not for charity
Except, maybe, for me.

It doesn't meet
On holidays or summer's heat.
But when color comes to trees
And football's in the breeze,
My club meets,
And, oh, what ease
I feel
As one by one I peel
My children from their beds
And straighten hair on sleepy
heads.
Then as they exit
Off to school
With faces washed
And tummies full
The house grows still (as my house
gets—
Save an occasional toddler's frets.)
Then my club meets
After weekend's din.
I pour another cup, and then—
Rejoice! The table's turning
And I'm so glad, at last, it's Monday
morning.

Consider the Lord's admonish-
ment, and regularly find a way to
rest a while.

REPUTATIONS ✴

*These sought their listing among those who were registered
by genealogy, but they were not found; therefore, they were
excluded from the priesthood as defiled. And the governor
said to them that they should not eat of the most holy things
until a priest could consult with the Urim and Thummim.*

EZRA 2:62-63

I was with great anticipation that I readied myself for Norwich High School's performance of *Phantom of the Opera*. NHS had a reputation for top notch drama. The previous year they had performed *Les Miserables*. It knocked me out.

That year, the production was *Phantom*. My son Ben was the auctioneer, among other parts, and the first one of the cast to speak. Theater was a new venture for him, and I was as proud as a mama could be.

"Why are all the car doors locked with the keys inside?" Cory asked early that Saturday afternoon. Cory has a reputation for joking around, but he wasn't kidding. No problem, I thought, we will just take the twelve-passenger van....a.k.a. Moby Dick, Jr.

Some new friends were joining us for appetizers from a nearby town, so I went about my day to prepare for their visit. Until I remembered my purse was in the car with the keys. And the tickets.

Last time I lost the keys, Captain Fun, who had a reputation for coming to my rescue, was able to use a coat hanger to get the door unlocked. He tried, but no such luck this time, he said, as the door that was slightly ajar last time was shut tight.

I texted another friend who had a reputation for empathy. *New complication: locked the keys in the car with the tickets.*

Do you have a spare? She texted back.

It's in my purse. In the car. With the tickets.

Then came the empathy I was looking for as she texted me her own story of locked car doors. *Is the car running? Silas is not in the car, is he?*

Silas, who has his own reputation, would have driven away in the van and picked up some friends from his preschool to take to the show. *No. He is inside with me. The car is in the garage. With the keys. And my purse. And the tickets.*

One thing I had learned about the NHS drama productions—they sold out every time. I thought about how I might convince the doorman that I bought my tickets weeks ago, hoping I had a reputation for honesty.

Maybe I could call one of the directors and explain, I thought, but I quickly decided against it. Disorganized people like myself can be very high maintenance—a reputation I didn't want to get in the little town.

My friends arrived and I showed them around. Then I came out with it. "I locked our tickets in the car. With the keys. And my purse." They went easy on me, perhaps because we were too newly acquainted for them to know my reputation.

No problem, I concluded. We would go earlier than planned and beg for more tickets. I didn't mind buying them twice, but at only $5.00 each for such quality theater, the show was certain to be sold out.

As I climbed into Moby II, I had the thought to look in the door's little cubby. Something shiny caught my eye.

It was, indeed, a key to the other van, which I had lost the previous fall. Of course, it makes perfect sense that it would be in the door of the twelve-passenger. If you're me, anyway.

When we arrived, the doorman was announcing the show was sold out. The line wound down the hall for what seemed like half a mile. But we got in. With our tickets. And my purse. And the keys.

Ben nailed it. In fact, the whole cast nailed it. The production was an absolute smash. Three shows, all sold out.

Norwich High School lived up to its reputation for excellence in theater. And, sadly, I lived up to my reputation of being very forgetful and disorganized, much like the sons of the priests in today's text. Boy, can I relate.

I regularly wish I was more together, orderly, organized and structured. I will never cease to be amazed by people who are naturally so. But meanwhile, I roll with it.

Yes, I get tired of my lost keys and my scatterbrained ways. I grow frustrated over how much longer everything takes because I so often have to backtrack. I really worry about the example I am setting for my kids.

But secretly I am hoping that they remember me not for my forgetful ways but for how I roll with the challenges of being absentminded. It is an issue I must face every single day, one I really have trouble overcoming. But I do my best, and I will never quit trying.

After all, what choice do I have? I have a reputation to keep, you know.

GOOD GUYS, BAD GUYS

Be sober, be vigilant; because your adversary the devil walks about like a roaring lion, seeking whom he may devour. Resist him, steadfast in the faith, knowing that the same sufferings are experienced by your brotherhood in the world.

1 PETER 5:8-9

With five boys, I have a lot of experience at playing good guys and bad guys. When Silas was three years old, he had unfortunately not yet mastered it.

Take one of the many times he had bumped his head on the kitchen counter, for instance. It jutted out at just the right place and height for him to catch it occasionally. "Grandmama pushed me!" he cried.

"Grandmama did not push you!" I said. "She would never do that. You need to say you're sorry."

"Sorry." How sincere.

Five minutes later. "Grandmama ate my yogurt!"

Sigh. May I take a moment to describe Silas's eating habits? He left his chicken nuggets and ate all his broccoli. He snubbed his fries and ate his salad. I've never experienced a preschooler with such a palate. An remember I have a lot to compare. If it was ice cream at stake, he wouldn't have cared. But this was his yogurt. His Fiber One Key Lime Pie yogurt.

"She did not eat your yogurt, Silas. You ate it."

"Noooo," he wailed. "Grandmama ate it."

Clearly, Silas had his allies and enemies confused, for if anyone was on his side, it was Grandmama. Toy Provider. Fan. Friend. Slave. Once, at his command, she put a Snapple box on her head and played robot with him. Then it was bowling in the hall with plastic cups for pins, and they watched TV in her bed while he ate his lunch, no matter that her sheets were filled with crumbs afterward. Grandmama, who stopped by the office door to tell me how terrific Silas was, and Silas stopped by fresh up from his nap to tell me I was a bad guy.

But don't we all do the same thing when challenges arise or life doesn't turn out the way we thought it would? Instead of recognizing our true enemy, we immediately blame the One who loves us the most.

Every so often I have to go retrieve Silas from Grandma's room. "Silas, I told you no more TV. And no candy either. It is too close to dinner."

"Grandmama said I could!"

"I confess," she always agrees. "He asked if he could watch and I couldn't resist."

Maybe he is better at this good guy, bad guy business than I give him credit for.

✦ONE TOUGH TASK

Now we exhort you, brethren, warn those who are unruly,
comfort the fainthearted, uphold the weak, be patient with
all. See that no one renders evil for evil to anyone, but always
pursue what is good both for yourselves and for all.

1 THESSALONIANS 5:14-15

Soon after our arrival in Virginia, I learned that one of my new friends from the bus stop had to have foot surgery. She had been in extreme pain for a long time, and when she finally went in for an x-ray she was shocked to discover her foot was broken. Not only was surgery a must, but the doctor also ordered no weight on the foot for over a month.

After the surgery, I met her husband, who had their baby in tow, at the bus stop. I introduced myself and told him I was bringing dinner over that weekend, and daughter Emma would be helping them out, to boot. He thanked me, seven-month-old in his arms, three-year-old around his leg, and his two other kids, kindergarten and first grade, in the bus line. He still had a smile on his face as he told us that until the in-laws arrived and he returned to work, he was playing Super Dad. He admitted uncertainty as to what his sanity status would be by then.

I told him I was a writer and warned it was going to be very hard for me not to document his temporary role. "Go right ahead," he said (I love it when people say that). He even added another detail just so I would have plenty to go on. "We have friends with five kids. She works, he stays home. Today I told her to go hug her husband." He laughed. The moms laughed. We all got it. Staying home with kids is hard.

"Warn the unruly, comfort the

fainthearted, uphold the weak," Paul urges the Thessalonians. Fits the job description of us moms, doesn't it?

A privilege? Yes.

A blessing? Yes.

A gift? Yes.

Easy? No.

I remember back when I was homeschooling my oldest three kids many years ago. It was my first year, and my September birthday fell on a school day. The same as I still frequently hear from my kids, I didn't want to do school on my birthday. Nothing they can do about it—public, private, or homeschool—they must go. I, on the other hand, had options. I called on Captain Fun. "Would you take a day off work so I can have my birthday off from school?"

He said he would be glad to. What else would Captain Fun say?

I shopped. I lunched. I'm sure I went to the bookstore and envisioned all the books I would someday write. (I confess, I still do that.)

When I came home, Captain Fun was still in his sweats from the night before. His hair was a wreck and he had spit up on his shirt. "I am exhausted," he said. "I did not sit down the entire day."

My hair was combed. My shirt was clean. I couldn't contain myself. I let out a laugh. A chuckle. Okay, a guffaw—which I immediately explained to the Captain. "You look like me, and I look like you." Though we hadn't exactly swapped roles (I had the day off instead of going to the office) we both roared with laughter. He is, after all, Captain Fun.

Since the Captain, himself, declared that staying home with small children is a challenge, that's all the proof I've ever needed. It has helped me stop comparing myself to other moms. Whether you stay at home or work outside the home, mothering is one tough task.

✦ KEEPING SCORE

*I thank my God upon every remembrance of you, always in
every prayer of mine making requests for you all with joy, for
your fellowship in the Gospel from the first day until now.*

PHILIPPIANS 1:3-5

I was doing my usual Saturday morning routine of cleaning everything in sight. With toilet brush in hand, I heard the familiar request.

"Play with us, Mom. You can be the general."

Sigh. "I can't. I am cleaning the bathrooms." Cory and Silas, in the middle of a game of battle, knew it was futile to ask again. Especially on Saturday morning.

As I swished the Comet around the toilet, an idea struck. I stepped out of the upstairs bathroom and peered over the railing, searching for my two little soldiers. "Captain Cory, here is a secret code." I moved my hand along the banister as if it were a sailing ship, then formed a half circle from left to right.

"Are you telling me to do my Saturday chores?" Cory asked.

"No, no, no. I am a soldier disguised as the maid," I retorted. "You said I was the general, remember? The secret signal means, 'We sail at sunrise.'"

"Oh, oh, oh. Come on, Private," he said to his little brother. They both disappeared.

Well, that was easy, I thought, feeling smug.

As I Windexed the mirrors and wiped down the sink, they reappeared.

"It is sunrise." Guess I would have to sail after all.

"Follow me, General, let's go get your gun," Cory ordered. I followed them into their room where I was promptly issued a Nerf gun. Cory then pulled out a piece of paper on which he had drawn the secret plans. Even though I was the commander, I followed orders.

Mom Dot, seated downstairs on the end of the couch, was the target. Cory counted to three, then the three of us rushed downstairs and hid behind the couch.

"I'm not believing this," she said when she saw me crouched behind the furniture, Nerf gun in hand. Sheer shock is often the reaction when someone sees me playing.

We redirected the mission when we saw Bethany heading our way. "Let's ambush Bethany when she comes in from out back," I ordered. The troops loved that idea. Bethany, accustomed to her brothers' ambushes, played along.

The mission took about five minutes. "Thanks for playing, Mom," Cory said. Music to a mother's ears. "You haven't played with me in two years." He could have left out that last part.

Really? Two years?

"Last time was when we played football in New York."

Oh.

That night when Captain Fun got home, we walked to the park. "Play football with us, honey," he said.

"No, thanks. I will swing Hope and you all can play." Besides, I thought, I have already met my two-year playing quota.

But, being the otter he is, Captain Fun wouldn't take "no" for an answer. It was the Captain and me against Mary and Cory. I don't remember who won, but I completed two passes. I must admit, it was fun.

I don't know why it is so hard for me to play, but I know I need to do more of it. I have heard many times that when the kids are grown, they won't remember how clean the house is. Now that three of my kids are grown, I know it really is true.

They will recall, however, whether I played with them. Unlike the football game in the park, they will remember the score.

✦ EGYPT OR BUST

*And you shall love the Lord your God with all your
heart, with all your soul, with all your mind, and with
all your strength. This is the first commandment.*

MARK 12:30

When Silas was four, my friend, Denise, gave him an Usborne book on Ancient Egypt. The first time he got his hands on it, he sat down and looked at it for a solid ninety minutes.

"Where is my Egypt book?" he regularly asked. If he cornered you with it in hand, you were doomed for the next hour to read to him about Ancient Egypt. "But don't show the mummy pages," he ordered.

"Tell Denise I am going to beat her with that book," Mom Dot teased. She was Silas's slave and would answer his every beck and call—even if it meant reading the same book every day.

"Let's teach about Egypt," Silas said one night after dinner. "What am I?" He laid down on the floor and crossed his arms.

"A mummy!" I said.

"Right! Now who am I?" he said, pointing to his chin, then bringing his hand down as if growing a beard.

"King Tut!" I said.

"That's right," he said. "Now what am I?" he asked, forming himself into a statue that I somehow guessed was a Sphinx. He was delighted.

A few days later he woke up crying from his nap, "I want to go to Egypt."

"It's too far away," I told him. "Let's just play Egypt." With some persuasion, he settled for pretending and reading his book.

I am originally from Memphis,

and when Silas spotted a picture of Memphis on my bathroom wall with a Pharaoh in the background, he was very excited. "An Egypt picture!" he exclaimed. I took it down. He took it to his room.

"Is that a pyramid?" he said soon after from the back seat of the van, pointing to the dollar bill Mom Dot was holding in the front seat. He was right. There is a pyramid on every dollar bill.

"Say it with me, Mom," Silas said one morning while getting dressed. "School, Egypt, home." I was fairly certain he was trying to trick me into taking a little detour on the way home from school that day.

Preschoolers are like sponges, someone said, soaking up everything they can. My homeschooling years taught me to take every opportunity that arises to teach my kids something. For weeks it was Egypt, next time (we all hoped) it would be something else.

Even when school isn't in session, keep teaching your kids, equipping them to love God with all their minds. Home school even if you don't homeschool, a friend told me once.

That's just good advice—no matter what the subject.

 SILAS'S DAY

Foolishness is bound up in the heart of a child;
the rod of correction will drive it far from him.

PROVERBS 22:15

W hen Silas was in preschool, an email appeared in my inbox with the subject line "Silas's Day." Silas, it seemed, had instigated a food fight at lunchtime. Would I speak to him?

I picked him up a little late and the after-school teacher was there. "He kissed a girl today," she said with a little smile.

On the way home I inquired about the kiss first. "Silas, did you kiss a girl today?"

"I kissed two girls," he answered. I forgot to ask about the other.

An hour after we got home, he came running. "Mommy! I made a puddle! I made a pee-pee puddle!"

"Where? Silas, you know how to use the potty."

"There," he said, pointing to the dog's bed. A puddle.

At dinner, he decided he would stand up in his chair and moon his brother Cory.

"Silas! You better cover that bare bottom up before I give it a swat."

He did, but then began a soliloquy. "Bare bottoms look like balloons. No, they look like bologna. Some animals have bare bottoms—crabs have bare bottoms, turtles have bare bottoms."

"Horses have bare bottoms," Mom Dot chimed in. Grandmothers are always helpful at times like this.

"Silas, do you want me to get Mr. Spanky?"

"Yes!" he threw both hands up in the air as if he had scored a buzzer beater during the Final Four.

"Spankings are fun!"

Ben and Cory's eyes got big as saucers. "The kid is an alien," I said. They agreed.

I picked him up, concealing my laughter. "Spankings are fun, spankings are fun," he chanted.

Once I got him to his room, he changed his mind about the humorous nature of spankings. "Come out when you can behave yourself at the dinner table," I told him.

He returned to the table shortly and everything was somewhat normal. Until the next day when I got another email from the teacher with that now familiar subject line.

This summary reported that he chose to go to the office rather than stop some rude behavior. I picked him up a little early so I could catch the teacher.

I made Silas apologize. "If he misbehaves again," I said, meaning it, "call me on my cell phone and I will very quickly appear."

"Thank you," she said.

"No, thank *you*," I replied.

That night and the next morning, I reminded Silas to be obedient. That if the teacher had to call me about his behavior, I was going to come up to the school and pick him up and there *would* be consequences. Guaranteed. The reminders worked, and the weeks following were uneventful. For Silas, anyway.

Silas is my ninth child—my fifth boy, no less. I don't know everything about raising kids, but for many years I have been very confident with parenting preschoolers. But that week I learned something. I was getting tired and, in my estimation, it is the parents who grow weary that throw up their hands and let the chips fall where they may.

I will be 60 years old when Silas leaves for college. But I am determined to finish the job of raising him right. Determined that whatever he dishes out—no matter how darn cute or funny he is—I will be there to remind him that I am in charge. Kids need that, I think.

"Just slap me if you see me letting Silas do whatever he wants," I told Bethany.

If that doesn't work, send me an email with the subject line "Silas's Day" and I will get right on it.

✳ HOW TO MAKE A MONSTER

*The rod and rebuke give wisdom, but a child
left to himself brings shame to his mother.*

PROVERBS 29:15

When Halloween rolls around, monsters come to mind. You may see one in the grocery store, the mall, or (as we all have occasionally) lurking about in your own home.

Whether you have one or ten kids, parenting is exhausting. It is a full-time job about which you must be relentless. But in case you're feeling too weary for the task, here is my recipe for creating your own little monster.

Homemade Monster

One heaping tablespoon (each) of sighs, cries and rolling of eyes.

Regular giant servings of every electronic gadget. For best results, add well before high school.

Frequent dashes of disrespect in the form of "none ya," "whatever," and "duh."

Serve the above with generous helpings of only what is desired at every mealtime.

Whip in a steady flow of popular culture—uncensored and unsupervised. Sprinkle in rudeness with pinches of bad sportsmanship and/ or bad manners.

Serving Suggestion: Steer clear of these last four ingredients for reaching maximum monster capacity, then follow the instructions below:

- Affordability: instead stream in a steady flow of cash.

- Accountability: never inspect what you expect.
- Reliability: require that no task ever be completed.
- Time: equal substitution: swap 1 hour time for 1 new toy/gadget.

Simmer for 18 years (or longer) at an even, steady temperature to prevent any and all discomfort.

Serving size: One Monster (but don't worry, there will be more than you bargained for).

After Halloween is over, most monsters will disappear. Follow this fool proof recipe, however, and you will have enough monster to last a lifetime.

✳ A SENSE OF HUMOR

Abraham and Sarah were old, well advanced in age; and Sarah had passed the age of childbearing. Therefore, Sarah laughed within herself, saying, 'After I have grown old, shall I have pleasure, my lord being old also?' Then the Lord said to Abraham, 'Why did Sarah laugh, saying, 'Shall I surely bear a child, since I am old?' Is anything too hard for the Lord? At the appointed time I will return to you according to the time of life, and Sarah shall have a son.' But Sarah denied it, saying, 'I did not laugh,' for she was afraid. And He said, 'No, but you did laugh.'

GENESIS 18:11-15

I knew before it ever happened that it would happen, and it didn't take long.

Hope was only two weeks old when I was out with my two teenage daughters, Mary and Emma. She was fussing while they shopped for clothes at our favorite consignment store. I told them I was going to take the baby outside. "That's right," a lady chimed in, "let Grandma take you outside." I flinched for half a second, but like I said, I saw it coming.

It is increasingly comical to me how many people mistake me for Hope's grandmother.

I once blogged about attending Matthew's "A" Day at West Point. Folks looked with awe at Matt in his West Point uniform, gazed softly at Hope in all her sweetness, then stared at the Captain and me, questions in their eyes. "Number three and number ten," we answered almost before they could ask.

And soon after Hope was born, the hair dresser just came right out and asked, "Is that your baby, or her baby?" as she gestured toward Bethany. At twenty-three, she was technically old enough to be Hope's mom. Which made me technically old enough to be Hope's grandmother. "They are both mine," I said with a laugh.

But it was when the checkout lady asked me if I wanted the senior discount for those fifty-five years or older that I stopped laughing. That wasn't funny. I gulped. I flushed red.

It really wasn't funny.

"You don't look fifty-five," both Bethany and Mom Dot reassured me on the way home. "It was only because I was with you," Bethany added. I found a little comfort in her words. I was, after all, still on the south side of fifty.

It was Hope I really felt sorry for. I could well imagine the conversations the first time she had a friend over to play: *Why do you live with your grandma?* Or at school when I brought cupcakes to her class for her birthday: *Why does your grandmother always come to school? Where is your mother?*

Then after she'd share the news that I was, in fact, her mother, the next question: *Why is your mother so old?*

Hope didn't know it yet, but there were advantages to having an older mother: I had more wisdom, for one thing, and more patience, as Cory pointed out when a plate crashed to the floor and I hardly noticed. "Stuff happens," was my only response.

The kids made observations frequently, in fact, of all the advantages she had being the youngest of ten. Hope would hardly ever have to take turns getting the front seat; Hope would have her own room way before she turned seventeen; Hope would be the only one at home for five years.

I prayed that Hope would have a strong sense of humor. Like her ancient mother, she was going to need it.

✳ MY RIGHT TO BE A REDHEAD

The silver-haired head is a crown of glory,
if it is found in the way of righteousness.

PROVERBS 16:31

When I was in first grade, I fell off the monkey bars and broke my left arm.

When I was in second grade, I tripped over my dog and broke my right arm.

"Redheads are smart, but they're clumsy," the doctor said as he was preparing the plaster for my shoulder length cast. My mother, also a redhead, cocked her head to one side. "Oh, pardon me," the doctor said.

In elementary school, the boys called me Carrot Top.

My sister (another redhead) gave me her shirt that said, "Orange eyelashes are cool."

In middle school, Coach Thomas regularly called me a red-headed pecker wood, whatever that meant. A teacher chanted daily, "I'd rather be dead than red on the head."

"Did you know," I asked my mother one day as a teenager, "that less than two percent of the world's population has red hair? I read it in a trivia book."

"Well, I have most of them, then," she laughed. Most of her eight kids were redheads. And like my mother, most of my kids are redheads. A mixed blessing.

"A boy called me a ginger today," my Mary said upon arriving home from school one afternoon. I thought I had heard every nickname for a redhead, but that one was new to me. "Get used to it," I said. "It is part of the package."

"I can never be truly happy," said

Anne Shirley in *Anne of Green Gables*. "No one can who has red hair."

Well, I wouldn't go that far. Being a redhead had been fun—until it suddenly wasn't anymore. "I wouldn't call you a true redhead," my longtime friend said to me over the phone one memorable day. "It has turned a more strawberry blond."

I had nothing against strawberry blond hair. It was just that my whole life I paid my dues for being a redhead. The freckles. The skin that won't tan. The orange eyelashes. The constant teasing. Now I'm a strawberry blond?

If you see me on the street, or if you have redheaded friends whose hair might be fading with age, don't mention it. Allow us to keep referring to ourselves as redheads.

After all, we've earned it.

✦DONE. WITH. DIAPERS.

Lo, children are a heritage of the Lord,
the fruit of the womb is a reward.
PSALM 127:3

I couldn't stop talking about it. I called my sisters. I called my friends. I Facebooked it, tweeted it, and told anyone who would listen. I was barely able to resist putting the news on my LinkedIn page, which seemed a bit unprofessional.

I started changing diapers in 1987. I did not quit until 2015.

Twenty. Eight. Years.

Done. With. Diapers.

Forgive me for stating the obvious, but my husband and I have chosen to accept all the children the Lord sends. Consequently, we have had constant simultaneous seasons at our house all these years, each requiring a sense of humor.

When our oldest son got engaged, for example, I had a secret fear that we would be expecting number ten by the time the wedding came. I could hear the whispers as the Mother of the Groom waddled in on the escort's arm.

To my relief, it didn't happen—until eighteen months later. "Mom," my son laughed, "I am closer in age to you than I am to my own sister." It's true, as I had him when I was twenty-one and he was almost twenty-five when Hope was born.

My daughter-in-law is the best with her great sense of humor. After all, how many new brides can say her mother-in-law is expecting? Becky is among the few.

When my husband and I went up to West Point for our second son's "A" Day, baby Hope was in the stroller. People looked at us, then at Hope, then at twenty year old Matthew. "Late in life surprise," I explained. Again, a sense of humor is required.

I posted the "Done with Diapers" news on a few large family Facebook groups in which I participated. I knew they would get how overjoyed I felt. And they did.

One mom of many actually showed me a resource to estimate just how many diapers I have changed.

And the answer? Approximately 51,323

That's fifty-one thousand, three hundred and twenty-three. The amount of money we've spent on diapers is probably somewhere around there, too.

A season, albeit a long one. But I have learned the end of one season will bring the beginning of another.

With a chuckle, I must add a verse that many a pastor has quoted from the pulpit. Paul is talking about how believers will not stay in the grave, but will be changed at the sound of the trumpet. "We shall not all sleep, but we shall all be changed." I Corinthians 15:51

The passage is one of great inspiration for those of us who are weary of this world, but it has come to mind many times over the years as I have changed a diaper in the middle of the night.

If you're in the trenches of diapers and sleepless nights, hang in there. The next season is coming.

 # UPWARD

I will lift up mine eyes unto the hills; from whence comes my help?
My help comes from the Lord who made Heaven and earth.

PSALM 121:1-2

As I write this last bit of wisdom, my oldest is thirty-two and my youngest is seven. Consequently, I am a little weary. As I enter this third decade of parenting, I have grown fond of a new (to me) phrase—Mom up.

When Hope was in swimming lessons for a few weeks, I told her I would get in and play with her while we waited for her teacher. Playing has never come easily to me (that's Captain Fun's department), but I knew what I had to do: suit up. Once her lesson began, as I was swimming my laps, I kept thinking of that word, up, and all the ways we moms might use it.

Here are some "up" words for you moms out there. May they come to mind at just the right time.

Got mileage? Tune up.

Isolated? Team up.

Feeling weary? Charge up.

Respect waning? Change up.

Hard on yourself? Let up.

Slacking off? Get up.

Clutching your old (pre-kid) freedoms? Give up.

Define the mom you want to be, then live up.

Kids need you—show up.

If you're stuck, grow up.

At the beach, suit up.

In the snow, boot up.

Once a day, feet up.

Back talk? Turn the heat up.

Tell your kids to line up,

and to put the whine up.

Require that they shine up.

In a hurry? Hold up.

Griping habit? Hush up.

Distracted mom? Heads up.

Made a mistake? Own up.

Screen head? Put the phone up.

All too soon they grow up.

I think one of my sons could put a rap beat to that.

Someone said motherhood goes from cop to coach to counselor to, finally, cheerleader. I have found that to be true in my journey.

Heads up, moms. Upward and onward. Don't let this culture raise your kids. Proverbs 29:15 reminds us "A child left to himself brings shame to his mother."

Motherhood is a marathon. Suit up. Show up. Mom up.

And above all, look up.

ACKNOWLEDGEMENTS

I am so grateful for the people who have never tired of my dream to write a book someday.

My husband, first and foremost, of course, who laughed at all the right places and has told me forever that I Absolutely. Could. Write. A. Book.

My children, who permit me to tell the stories.

My mother, who hung my articles on the fridge until the day she died.

My dad, who made me feel like I was good at everything. Well, except math.

My five sisters, who listened to my dream and always cheered me on. Baby loves you.

My mother-in-law, Mom Dot, who always told me I had that "creative yeast" that writers must have to see a project through to completion.

Jane Schneider, my friend, writing coach, and editor (in that order) of twenty years, who taught me nearly everything I know about writing. Our friendship formed effortlessly in the process. Thank you.

My editor, Allison Marlow, who gave me my first parenting column in *The Fairhope Courier*. Thank you for believing in me. I know God guided me to sit down beside you at the elementary school auction meeting that Tuesday morning.

My publisher's CEO, Kim Vogel Sawyer, with whom I immediately connected at the Blue Lake Writer's Retreat. After two decades of no's, thank you for being the one who said yes.

My book editor, Connie Stevens, who so carefully kept my voice. Working with you has been a delight.

To my cousin and cover illustrator, Sally Bennett Baxley, an accomplished, talented, even famous artist who "wasn't sure" she was "a good illustrator" but was "willing to give it a go." Your work took my breath away. Thank you for giving it a go.

Thank you to everyone who invited me to speak in faraway places from Vermont to Italy:

To my sister Sherry, who gave my confidence a huge boost by asking me to lead a retreat for the very first time. To my friend Joan, who invited me to speak at your women's events every chance you got (not to mention taking care of Bethany all through college). To Lyn and Rachel, who kept inviting me back to Vermont; and Lauren, for for getting me to Italy *(Italy!)* to speak at the PWOC retreat. Finally, Lea, thanks for the hours you spent on the phone encouraging me during the many silent seasons when my writing/speaking so frequently came to a halt.

To my friends at Essex Alliance Church, Essex, Vermont. Even though our kids (or at least, for me, *that* set of kids) are grown, the connection between us remains. I will never forget how you welcomed this twangy southerner into your hearts all those years ago. And over a decade later when my sisters said half the state of Vermont was at Matt's wedding? I knew they were right.

To the whole wonderful group of women and my women's ministry team at Parkway Baptist, Moseley, Virginia. Your easy friendship and your affirmation of my leadership strengthened my faith in more ways than you can know. Thank you.

To the MOPS group at Fairhope United Methodist. Thank you for inviting me to speak and then asking me to stay on as Mentoring Mom and Bible study teacher. You have shown me that it truly doesn't matter that I am twenty years older than most preschool moms out there—the love we have for our children is our common ground.

To the moms I've encountered at the playground, MOPS groups, the grocery store, the doctor's office. Thanks for asking for advice "because you have ten kids." You helped convince me that moms everywhere both needed and wanted this book.

To the "Jesus Girls" at First Baptist Silverhill, my cheerleaders. You showed up just when I needed someone to tell me how to do the next season of life.

You all helped me believe I had something to say.

Est. 2013

Wings of Hope Publishing is committed to providing quality Christian reading material in both the fiction and non-fiction markets.